Charles R. Lorrai
executive director
International Conference of Pol

Chaplain Nolta gives us a raw and honest look at what it "costs" to care and be compassionate in ministry. Whether one is in the law enforcement chaplaincy profession or someone simply reading for general interest, Nolta has given each the unique ability to enter in and "feel" what a chaplain experiences through his own personal journey.

I would highly recommend this book to anyone who is contemplating going into ministry. It well serves as a benchmark for the cost of caring and demonstrates both sides of what it takes to be a good chaplain as well as the painful price paid for the privilege. It is a wonderful tool as a proactive measure in maintaining chaplaincy health and wellness.

Arthur O. Roberts
professor at large
George Fox University

Dan Nolta weaves his personal spiritual journey into stories of human tragedy and redemption drawn from his many years of police chaplaincy. With poignancy and candor he offers a compelling witness to both the joys *and the costs* of a Christian ministry of compassionate caring. I found evocative and enriching a secondary theme: how timely words from discerning friends at transitional moments open a door for the Holy Spirit to bring healing and peace to troubled folks.

Because of this book I will try to be more understanding and appreciative of persons, uniformed or otherwise, who respond to tragic events day after day. May the God of all comfort be a comfort to them when they feel burned out or traumatized by violence!

COMPASSION

THE PAINFUL PRIVILEGE

by Dan Nolta

BARCLAY PRESS

COMPASSION
THE PAINFUL PRIVILEGE

© 2006 by Dan Nolta

Published by
BARCLAY PRESS
Newberg, OR 97132

www.barclaypress.com

Unless otherwise indicated all scriptural quotations
are from the *Holy Bible: New International Version.*

International Standard Book Number: 1-59498-004-7

Cover design by Dan Jamison
Printed in the United States of America

To my beloved parents, **Vance and Maxine**,
who loved me and taught me through hard times.
After their divorce they each remarried,
and gave me a whole bunch of siblings
(**Big Bill, Mike, Sue, Scott, Don, Roger, Little
Bill, and Clint**)... "my kids, your kids, and our kids."

To my wife, **Judi**, and my children—
Julie, Jeff, Daven, Darci, Dixie, and **Rene**—
all of whom so patiently, lovingly, and without complaint
shared me for so many years.

To my spiritual parents and life mentors—
Clynton and Marjorie Crisman and
Dr. Wayne and Bertie Roberts.

To all of you readers
who are yourselves gifted with compassion
and who deliver it in the spirit of
Sam Shoemaker's poem,
"I Stand by the Door":

I stand by the door.
I neither go too far in, nor stay too far out.
The door is the most important door in the world—
It is the door through which men walk when they find God.

....

Men die outside that door, as starving beggars die
On cold nights, in cruel cities, in the dead of winter.
Nothing else matters compared to helping them find it,
And open it, and walk in, and find Him.
So, I stand by the door.

....

You can go in too deeply and stay in too long,
And forget the people outside the door.

As for me, I shall take my old accustomed place,
Near enough to God to hear Him, and know He is there,
But not so far from men as not to hear them,
And remember they are there too.

Where? Outside the door—
Thousands of them. Millions of them.
But—more important for me—
One of them, two of them, ten of them.
Whose hands I am intended to put on the latch.
So I shall stand by the door and wait
For those who seek it.
"I had rather be a door-keeper..."
So I stand by the door.

CONTENTS

No one writes a book alone. Whether by spoken words or silent demonstration, others have contributed to the pieces that make up the whole. In recognition of what others have contributed to the thoughts conveyed in these words and to the emotion behind them, I say thank you to:

- my family, especially to my wife, Judi, who has shared my time with others...once again.

- Medford Friends Church who loved me to the Lord and became my "other family," and especially Pastor Clynton Crisman and his wife, Marjorie, and Dr. Wayne and Bertie Roberts, whose unflagging love, mentoring, and care set an example for me of what it means to love people.

- author and provider of self-understanding for me, Henri Nouwen, for his books *The Wounded Healer* and *Compassion: A Reflection on the Christian Life.*

- the author who made Christianity make sense to me, E. Stanley Jones, for his book *Is the Kingdom of God Realism?*

- all of my fellow chaplains inside and outside of the International Conference of Police Chaplains who have shared the "bitter pills" with me on so many dark nights.

- Lyle Smith, now-retired chief of the Tacoma Police Department, who risked a lot and gave a group of us pastors a chance to be his chaplains.

- all of the men and women of the Pierce County Sheriff's Department who allowed me to serve them for twenty years. Thank you for the privileges you extended to me.

⋄ my unofficial editor and sister, Sue, who transcribed every newsletter I wrote and made it possible for people to access them electronically and who encouraged me and gave me some great ideas when my own were in doubt.

⋄ Dan McCracken, longtime friend and publisher of Barclay Press, who way back in 1988 wrote me a letter and said, "You need to write a book." Dan, you put Barclay's money where your mouth is, gave me a very capable and compassionate editor, Tracy Sumner, and, by doing all of this, gave me the chance to share my heart.

I could feel the sting—and my defenses going up—as I read the letter from my good friend Gil, a former missionary and now a pastor, a position I had held before I became a police chaplain. I had written an article for our church magazine challenging Christians to "pry their hands off their eyes" and get out into the "real world" and see the things I was seeing as a police chaplain— out where God was *really* needed. Gil lovingly typed me off this private response:

> I submit to you that to see "life the way it really is," one would be better off to stay in the pastorate than to seek such in other ways. Are the problems that pastors deal with any less real because there are no sirens or lights flashing, though most pastors have been involved in many of those kinds of events as well?...I believe in you, and I believe in the ministry you are performing as a chaplain. But let me leave you with a standing invitation that if at any time you decide you would like to have the hands pried off your eyes and experience life the way it really is, I'm sure we can find a place for you as a pastor. I'm smiling, Dan...honest, I'm smiling!

As I read these words I felt his indignation over my air of superiority in the spiritual "pecking order." *Well, I didn't*

Isaiah 40:1-2

*Comfort, comfort
my people,
says your God.

Speak tenderly
to Jerusalem,
and proclaim to her
that her hard service
has been
completed,
that her sin has been
paid for,
that she has received
from the Lord's
hand
double for all her
sins.*

mean it like that...or did I? I thought. *Do I really think I am the only one out there exercising the gift of compassion...that I am "doing it right" but others are not? Have I developed such an air of spiritual superiority that others, including my own friends, are beginning to talk about it among themselves?*

All of that whirled through my mind as I read Gil's letter. Though it was gently worded, and from a friend who cared about me, I got the point. I was not the only one doing God's work. Others were doing real, compassionate ministry as well.

Now feeling thoroughly chastened, I realized that my appointed ministry is just that—my *appointed* ministry. It was where God has planted me, and it was where I had the privilege of loving people for his sake. It was God who had so graciously given me the wonderful gift of compassion, and it was God who had appointed me as a police chaplain. From that position, I had exercised that gift. And I hadn't done it any *better* than anyone else—just differently.

I had started my years of ministry as a very new Christian. I had become a pastor right out of college, too eager to get started in ministry to be bothered with getting more education. That would have to come later.

Still fairly new in the pastorate, I volunteered to be a police chaplain. It was then that I entered into an intoxicating world where adrenaline is the "drug of choice" for guys like me. Now, some thirty-five years later, I can look back at my years in that particular ministry and think of all I have come to know and believe about the God of compassion who gifts his children with compassion. I have realized that God gifts his children that way so that others may be blessed with the presence of those who are willing to suffer with them the insults, the tragedies, and the pain that life so often deals out.

I have also learned that for every person who has the gift of compassion, God provides a "life context" in which that person can carry out compassionate acts for the good of others. For those appointed to ministries like mine, these contexts are often filled with crisis, tragedy, suffering, and sometimes death. Within my God-appointed role as a police chaplain I have been privileged to act as a compassionate helper both to victims and to those dedicated to assisting them—the men and women who work in the police and fire services.

2 Corinthians 1:2-4

Grace and peace to you from God our Father and the Lord Jesus Christ. Praise be to the God and Father of our Lord Jesus Christ, the Father of compassion and the God of all comfort, who comforts us in all our troubles, so that we can comfort those in any trouble with the comfort we ourselves have received from God.

Relatively speaking, few are called to exercise compassion as police chaplains. But that doesn't mean there aren't countless opportunities, even for the "layperson," to demonstrate compassion in this world so full of tragedy and suffering. For the typical Christian, opportunities to demonstrate compassion may present themselves in "everyday" situations, such as comforting a next-door neighbor suffering from cancer, offering kind words and encouragement to a friend who is going through a painful divorce, or letting a child who wanders aimlessly around the neighborhood know that there is a friend who truly cares whether he or she lives or dies.

As my friend Gil so lovingly pointed out, compassion isn't always exercised in the context of "front-page drama." It is sometimes demonstrated just as effectively in "just between you and me" situations. Compassion exercised is the neighbor who sees a family without enough food and provides a pot of chicken and dumplings for dinner. Compassion exercised is the public school teacher who senses the neediness of her second-grade student and makes sure he gets to Sunday school. Compassion exercised is the family who loves a needy young man so much they dip into their own funds to anonymously provide a scholarship so he can go to college. Compassion exercised is a "veteran" minister mentoring a struggling young pastor so that he finds his way and is able to minister effectively. Compassion exercised is giving support to one God has called into a faith ministry.

I personally know the value of exercising these kinds of acts of compassion because they were all lovingly showered upon me during my lifetime. I know that without them, I wouldn't be where I am today.

Whatever the context, God's work of compassion is done because people, the crown of his creation, interact— helper and helpee, victim and rescuer—and share in need and in the weight of suffering.

If we as Christians want to see a perfect picture of one who demonstrated God's compassion, we need look no further than the Gospels—the four books of the Bible that tell the story of the life and ministry of Jesus Christ. Jesus was the ultimate Helper and Rescuer because he was perfectly obedient to the will of his Father, who had sent him to rescue the lost and provide them a way to have fellowship with God.

Of all Jesus' demonstrations of compassion, I am drawn to this profound story found in Matthew's Gospel:

> As Jesus and his disciples were leaving Jericho, a large crowd followed him. Two blind men were sitting by the roadside and when they heard that Jesus was going by, they shouted, "Lord, Son of David, have mercy on us!" The crowd rebuked them and told them to be quiet, but they shouted all the louder, "Lord, Son of David, have mercy on us!" Jesus stopped and called them. "What do you want me to do for you?" he asked. "Lord," they answered, "we want our sight." Jesus had compassion on them and touched their eyes. Immediately they received their sight and followed him. (*Matthew 20:29-34*)

Philippians 2:1-3

If you have any encouragement from being united with Christ, if any comfort from his love, if any fellowship with the Spirit, if any tenderness and compassion, then make my joy complete by being like-minded, having the same love, being one in spirit and purpose. Do nothing out of selfish ambition or vain conceit, but in humility consider others better than yourselves.

This instructive story draws us in with its simplicity. We can apply its principles to situations that prompt us to exercise compassion.

This book is thus devoted to those traveling down the road of life with their own Jericho in their "rearview mirror." It is devoted to those who—though they are surrounded by noisy, clamoring crowds—hear the voice of one in need and, instead of just moving on to get to the destination on time, stop to get involved, hear the need, be moved with compassion, and reach out and touch.

To hear the voice of one in need is one thing, but to stop and confront the source of the voice is quite another. To allow yourself to be pulled into the suffering of the "blind" one is yet another. And finally, to reach out and touch is compassion exercised. The rheumy eyes—swollen, red and runny, crusty with the discharge of infection—you reach out and touch them, and to do so is a painful privilege.

The arena for the exercise of compassion is different for each of us, and likewise, the crowd that clamors for our attention is different also. For you, the clamoring crowd may be the cry of your child who needs a diaper change, the harried work to get dinner on the table so Junior can get to ball practice on time and spouse can get to the church meeting. It may be the long list of phone calls or e-mails waiting to be answered or another deal waiting to be closed. It may be a sermon that needs to be written for Sunday morning, and it is already Saturday. For many, this "clamoring crowd" can drown out the voices of the "blind" around you and compete for the time it takes for you to get "involved."

But for those who are truly gifted with a compassionate spirit, the clamor is never loud enough to completely shut out the cries of those in need. And the needy are never so unlovely or unclean that you do not stop beside the road, reach down to them, and apply the gentle touch.

Those who find themselves frequently hearing, stopping, and touching know (as I do) that it can make for a very expensive "side trip" in life. To get involved in sharing the pain of another is indeed costly. The hours given, sleep disturbed, and vicarious pains endured are all parts of the cost paid as we emulate Jesus, the "man of sorrows and acquainted with grief" (Isaiah 53:3 KJV).

Those who have made hearing, stopping, and touching a way of life will discover the great rewards that come as the Lord showers back into their own lives the love given, the mercy shown, and the compassion demonstrated. They will personally enjoy a richness in their lives as well as the deep assurance they are divinely privileged to be a blessing and gift for those in need and suffering. God has chosen some of us and entrusted us with the responsibility of crossing the yellow "crime scene tape" in the lives of others and standing with them in their pain.

If that resonates in your heart, then this book was written for you.

> Matthew 25:35-36
>
> *"For I was hungry and you gave me something to eat, I was thirsty and you gave me something to drink, I was a stranger and you invited me in, I needed clothes and you clothed me, I was sick and you looked after me, I was in prison and you came to visit me."*

CHAPTER 1

My Defining Moment

From the very day I began my work as a chaplain for the Tacoma Police Department, I had no doubt that God had somehow brought me to this place. I just knew he had combined all my past life experiences—including my redemption and giftedness—and chosen this specific place as my appointed place of service.

Police chaplaincy became for me a divine appointment, and I found it necessary to at all times keep that fact in front of me as I entered into the heady world of the power and authority wielded by the police. To carry their ID, wear clothing items stamped with the word *police*, and ride with them as they responded to calls or arrived at violent crime scenes I found exciting. It was, to be honest, "adrenaline junky" stuff.

If I had failed to constantly remind myself that this place and ministry was my divine appointment, I could easily have been caught up and drowned in badges, pins, radios, lights, and sirens and become nothing more than a cop "wannabe." I would have negated all the good God was doing through me. If I had fallen into that trap, I would have been doing the right things but for the wrong reasons.

If each of us has a divine appointment—and I believe with my whole heart that we do—then we have as well, within each of our personal experiences, a defining moment. That one instant or incident establishes our commitment to doing the right things for the right reason. We can then rejoice, not feeling we have "arrived," but knowing we have found our place of service for God's kingdom. Only then can we be certain we are in the place God has appointed for us and in the time he has designed for us to be there.

My defining moment came in 1985. What follows is a combination of my best recollections, results of interviews, and police reports of what has become known as the "Spanaway Junior High Incident." With nationwide impact, it was likely the first widely chronicled killing of students by another student. Now eclipsed by the horror of Columbine and other incidents of its kind, it was nevertheless a first: painful on-the-job training for police and school administrators alike in the "how-to school" of dealing with on-campus tragedy. But for me it was more. It began my marriage to the Pierce County (Washington) Sheriff's Department. At that defining moment I knew beyond a doubt that I would be alongside these men and women for the rest of my working career. We were married; we belonged together. I described that horrific incident in my regular newsletter to friends and financial contributors.

On November 27, 1985, I wrote

Dear Friends across America:

The kids have shouted and romped enjoying the days out of school...snow is always like that. It excites kids. They roll in it, throw it, and love the moments of freedom it provides. But last night was different. It was kids in the snow, but it was all wrong.

She was lying on her back with blood streaming from her ears and mouth. Frantic paramedics and police personnel worked over her trying to make her live. Only fourteen years old!

At about 1630 hours I heard the call of two kids shot at Spanaway Junior High. I didn't respond immediately because I knew it would be a bad call. Junior high kids don't get shot on snowy afternoons in November! Junior high kids play in the snow, hold hands, laugh, have emotional highs and lows, and worry about pimples. The report came, "We have two down at the school."

It seemed an eternity before I could navigate the sixteen miles in the snow and traffic. I was greeted by the lieutenant and asked to inform Gordy's mom that he was dead...he was the one who was lying in the snow outside the gym...no longer concerned about wrestling practices, his new skis, or Boy Scouts. Chris was at Madigan Hospital never to regain consciousness, his organs to be donated to someone who wanted life as much as he did. And Heather...somewhere still packing that lethal little .22 rifle.

Things began to calm somewhat and then it happened. A teenager came over and asked, "You're looking for a girl with a rifle, aren't you? I saw her at the Taco Bell a half hour ago." Another came, "You're looking for a girl with a rifle, aren't you? She's coming this way." People scattered for the gym. The media, with cameras flying, hardly knew whether to run or stand and record it all.

Our deputies quickly formed a perimeter. Then, it was just Heather and the whole world. Heather and the whole world of her private pain that will never be understood by anyone else...not her parents, not her friends, and not the deputies who faced her across fifty feet of snowy parking lot. "Heather, put down the gun! Heather, let's talk about it. Heather, be reasonable." But Heather's moments of reasonable and rational thought are over.

A .22 doesn't make much noise. No one except those close even heard the shot, just the cry for fire medics. I ran that way, not yet believing she had shot herself.

She's just a little girl! A body bundled against the snowy weather now stripped of coat and sweater as CPR is begun. Deputies now stand with little to do except mourn...mourn the

junior high kids that should be playing in the snow on a
November afternoon.

◇

Heather, Gordon, and Christopher (I have left out all the
last names in this story) had come along an unchosen path,
following their family moves from place to place, career choice
to career choice. They came through different grade schools
but were finally brought together that fateful day, first by junior high "puppy love" and then by anger-filled but purposeful
choices that ended in tragic circumstances.

What is left today, some twenty years later, are the bitter-
sweet memories of young teens beginning their lives. Pictures
on the wall yet evoke tears from parents who remember their
innocent, chubby-cheeked children, and the pain of what happened one fateful day in November 1985.

The life journeys of others also brought them to that day.
We did not lose our lives, but in some strange mixing of tragedy and the privileged appointment of being there—on scene
where these three teens' fates clashed—our lives were forever
changed.

My Own Journey

I loved being a pastor, but nothing seemed to compare or
"click" like that first ride-along I took with the Tacoma Police
Department on January 2, 1971. Somehow, I knew from that
moment that I was on a divine appointment and destined to
work alongside the men and women of law enforcement.

The early "Crisis Clergy" program had taken a new step,
and we had approached Tacoma Police Chief Lyle Smith to see
if we could increase our exposure to crisis incidents by riding
with his officers on Friday and Saturday nights. In a bold
move, he said, "Yes." Despite the assertion by Captain Grady
that "the damn program won't work," we were in the door.

(Years later, Captain Grady was gone, and we chaplains were by then firmly accepted by the citizens and, more importantly, by the officers themselves.)

God had patiently and gently guided me through seven years at the Tacoma Police Department before I decided to leave the TPD to devote more time to kids and church. The daunting challenge of learning to balance leading a growing church, raising five growing children, and meeting the increasing demands of coordinating an expanding chaplaincy program finally made me pull in my horns and say "Enough!"

But I knew that God's personal promise to me—"Delight yourself in the Lord and he will give you the desires of your heart. Commit your way to the Lord; trust in him and he will do this" (Psalm 37:4-5)—would one day be fulfilled. That promise assured me I would be back in the chaplaincy, and back I was. In God's perfect timing, I gave four years to the Tacoma Fire Department chaplaincy.

That cold, wintry afternoon of November 26, 1985, I was once again under divine appointment—in my second year as a full-time chaplain for the Pierce County Sheriff's Department. The day had been filled with normal chaplaincy stuff. I had gone home early to be Dad and later drove my youngest daughter, Dixie, to music lessons—with one ear attuned to the portable radio I carried with me. I heard the alert tone and then, "Pierce County units, report of two students down at Spanaway Junior High, 15701 East B Street. The shooter is believed to still be in the area." My first thought was, *Oh, that's a bogus call. Kids don't get shot at school.*

A few minutes later, I knew I was wrong. "Pierce County units: confirmed we have two students down." I had just dropped Dixie off for her lesson when I heard the request that would forever make me a different person: "Pierce County Unit 990, respond to Spanaway Junior High."

"990 responding from northeast Tacoma," I answered.

"990, can you give us an ETA [estimated time of arrival]?"

My mind quickly estimated the distance and the late-afternoon traffic with the snow on the ground, and I knew it would be a problem. I wanted to be there; I wanted to help. But it was so far. Two students shot, the shooter still on the loose, the awful gathering of people, and me at least thirty minutes away. I drove as quickly as I could in my personal car, with no emergency equipment to speed my way.

"Pierce County Unit 990, how long till you will get here?" I heard over the radio, and I knew that the situation was serious. They weren't requesting more units; they were requesting the chaplain. I was the "new kid on the block," and the officers barely knew me. I was just making my way into the department, meeting people, raising support, developing some new volunteers, and just setting up for the first major crisis.

This *was* that crisis!

Heather

The snow crunched under her feet, so warmly clad in her "moon boots" that were the rage with the girls those days. School was out for the day and the welcome Thanksgiving holiday came later that week. Despite her short stature—she stood only five feet, one inch tall—Heather strode quickly home as if on a mission.

She was on a mission!

Gordon can't do this to me! He can't be paying attention to other girls. All the girls will laugh at me. I told them I would do it and now I will. If I can't have him, no other girl can have him either. I'll go get a gun at home and I will shoot him just like I said. If anyone gets in my way I will shoot them too. He can't do this to me!

Heather, a pert and bouncy fourteen-year-old cheerleader who had been a designated and trained Natural Helper (peer counselor), quickly took the little Ruger 10/22 rifle from its cabinet. The plan was only a couple of phone calls away from being irretrievably set in motion.

Heather called Betty and Patricia, and they quickly came the few blocks to her house. The plan was so often repeated that it had become a work of fiction not to be believed. One more time—one more *fatal* time—they did not believe. She had told Casey and Trudy, the other two parts of this trio of girls who imagined one another as best friends. They had talked of suicide together, and Heather had even cut her wrist the month before. She had talked to a school counselor as well as to a doctor at the hospital. She had talked to her parents and, finally, to her two friends. And still no one took her as seriously as they would in a few minutes. Now, just a half-hour before the culmination of the deadly plan, even Heather's loading of the rifle and shooting it into the fireplace did not convince these girls that this time she meant business.

The plan: Get Gordy alone and kill him. If anyone interfered, she would kill them too. Heather's grand finale would be to kill herself. She had tried that before, and now she would do it.

You are going to see things my way. Everyone *will see things my way.*

But how could she get the gun to school without carrying it through the streets? After wrapping it in an afghan, she began calling her older friends from the high school asking for a ride. Scott couldn't do it, so she called Shane. He would be right over. With a quick "I love you very much. Take care," to little brother Mike, she got into Shane's car. Only one short stop at Casey's house and only one word uttered: "Goodbye."

"Heather, what do you mean, 'Goodbye'?" Casey asked.

"Goodbye," Heather responded, and in another two minutes she was on the killing grounds of Spanaway Junior High School.

Chris

Chris's last word was most likely *Please!* It came as he stepped between Gordy and Heather. He never had a chance to finish his sentence. Now, the deadly little rifle was no longer pointed at Gordy. Now, it was pointed at him.

What are friends for? Chris and Gordy were both members of the wrestling team. Chris was half a head shorter, five-foot-two and weighing in at just 110 pounds. With wrestling practice finished and showers taken, these two buddies, dressed against the cold, snowy late afternoon, exited the gym.

For Chris, the argument with Heather at the door of the gym was over. She had bothered his buddy enough. What girl in her right mind still pursues a guy four or five months after they have split up? *Heather does.* Why doesn't she wise up and leave Gordy alone like Chris had just told her? "Don't bother him anymore."

That should have ended it, but it did not.

Heather was not going to stop "bothering" Gordy. As Gordy and Chris rounded the corner of the gym heading out toward the street, Heather came striding with deadly purpose, her moon boots crunching in the snow, leaving tracks later to be measured and compared. In her hands was the rifle. She quickly leveled it at Gordy.

Chris quickly stepped between Heather and Gordy. In Heather's mind, it was Chris standing in the way—literally—of the plan.

I told them I would probably have to kill him too. He can't stop me!

The last words before the little rifle cracked off the first two shots: "Put down the gun, Heather. You don't want to do this. Just put it down, *please...*"

The first body in the snow was Chris's. Chris, the loving son and good big brother and friend, was transported to Madigan Army Hospital trauma unit, where some five hours later he became an organ donor that others might live when he could not.

Gordon

For junior high boys and girls, the courtship ritual usually goes like this: "I like her. Does she like me? Tell her and see what she says." Then two weeks later it's over. She has a new interest and so does he—life goes on.

But somehow it didn't work that way this time. It had been several months, and Gordy thought it was over. But as soon as Heather saw him paying attention to another girl, she became very angry. The rumors had flown around Spanaway Junior High that she had been pregnant, that she was going to get even...and she was in another snit this afternoon.

Heather had never come to the gym looking for him before, and Gordy was glad that Chris had headed her off. With wrestling, Scouts, homework, and all that kind of stuff, he hardly had time for girls. For now, all he wanted to do was get home and have something to eat, hit the books, and get to bed.

Chris and Gordy had just exited the back door of the gym and come around the corner when they saw her standing there. This time, however, something was different. Heather was carrying a rifle. With anger on her face and in her voice, she raised the rifle and aimed it right at his head. In a flash, Chris was there in front of Gordy, moving in to block the shots that were sure to come. The final plea, the shots, and then...Chris was out of the way. Gordy and Heather stood all alone. No smiles, no coy behavior, no flirting—just the anger. Gordy turned to run, but it was too late. The first shot to his head felled him, and two more quickly followed.

This tragic junior high romance was over in a few deadly seconds. All that remained for Heather was to complete her plan. The final shot fired that day would come soon.

Bob

Lieutenant Bob had been a member of the Pierce County Sheriff's Department for only nine years, but he was well on his way to the top. A good test taker, Bob was on the captain's list in as brief a time as the regulations allowed. His military experience in Vietnam, his leadership ability, and the fact that he was a big guy—standing about six-foot-five—truly put him head and shoulders above many in the department.

It all counted that afternoon as he sat in the precinct in Lakewood. His position as lieutenant often kept him in the office unless there was a major event, and this one sounded major all right. Lights and sirens leading the way, he quickly arrived for field management at the shooting scene. Bob led the field personnel of the Pierce County Sheriff's Department for the next two hours. Detectives, administrative personnel, forensics, and chaplains all did their respective jobs, creating order out of chaos and sense out of a nonsensical tragedy.

Bob's matter-of-fact report didn't come close to capturing his feelings about what had happened that day.

Bob's report

At 1820 Unit 189, Mike, and I were in the school's administration offices talking with school personnel and Captain Mark when an unknown school employee came in stating that Heather had been seen in front of Thompson Elementary. Unit 189 and I went out the west-facing entrance of Spanaway JHS and walked N/B toward Thompson Elementary. I observed a W/F matching

Heather's description walking S/B along the W side of Thompson Elementary. I could see that the subj. was carrying what appeared to be a rifle. When the subject reached the SW corner of Thompson Elementary and stepped into the alleyway between Thompson and Spanaway JHS, I called the name "Heather" and told her to walk toward us (Mike and me). Heather took one step forward and raised the rifle to her head...Mike and I were both yelling repeatedly, "Don't do it!" and Heather lowered the gun. I told Heather to put the gun down and that everything would be alright. She said, "No, it won't," and raised the gun to her head again...I locked my service revolver in single-action and took a two-hand support over the roof-line of a parked vehicle. Heather lowered the rifle again and we continued to talk to her, trying to get her to put the gun down. Heather once again raised the rifle to her temple and immediately pulled the trigger. She immediately fell, dropping the weapon.

Unit 189 and I ran to the girl and, rolling her from her side onto her back, began C.P.R. I administered mouth to mouth resuscitation while Unit 189 did C.P.R. Heather had so much blood in the nasal passage and throat that I had difficulty maintaining an open airway. We continued C.P.R. until relieved by medical personnel.

I taped off the scene for preservation of evidence and placed Unit 240 as security. Heather was transported to Madigan via ambulance.

Nothing further at this time.

◇

Heather, Christopher, and Gordon were dead. For them, life on earth, with its boyfriend/girlfriend junior high crushes, wrestling practices, and Boy Scouts was over. But for Bob and Mike and all the others on scene at Spanaway Junior High, the aftermath of what had happened that day was just beginning.

For Bob, it was the beginning of the end. A traumatic Vietnam assignment, a secret drug habit brought back with him from his tour, the stress of working as a policeman, and the tragic death of a little girl brought this giant of a man down.

Despite the counseling, the inpatient posttraumatic stress disorder treatment program, and the support of his family and friends, Bob's career in law enforcement, as well as his marriage, would in time dissolve.

An Unbreakable Bond

While the Spanaway Junior High incident was the beginning of the end of Lieutenant Bob's law enforcement career, it was for me the beginning of a "till death do us part" marriage to the sheriff's department.

I witnessed Bob and Mike and Dick form the perimeter to keep the rest of us safe from this little girl and her deadly rifle—one moment protecting us from her and the next rushing to her side in a futile effort to save her life. I witnessed those things, and I *knew*. I knew that moment—and in the days to come as I witnessed the compassion and caring of the sheriff's department poured out on students, faculty, and parents—that I wanted to be a part of this wonderful law enforcement agency. It was my "defining moment." It confirmed that I did indeed belong here and that I was to be part of the mission these deputies and their leaders carried out.

Here I could freely practice a ministry of compassion and be welcomed, understood, and encouraged by these men and women who too often appear so cynical and hardened. Here, in an agency whose core values include compassion for people, I would fit right in.

I believe that each of us who have been given the wonderful gift of compassion will also receive from God a context in which we can exercise it for the good of others. For me, it was the sheriff's department. For some, it may be working on the international scene assisting refugees. Or it might be working as a volunteer in a local hospice or food bank. For others it may simply be working in their neighborhoods to make their neighbors' lives better and pain easier to bear.

To all of my brothers and sisters in Christ who desire to exercise their gift of compassion, I say this: There is that special place for each of us to do just that.

God wonderfully works through his written Word, through life circumstances, and through past experiences to guide us to that place where we can best serve and exercise our gifts for him. And I believe that if we ask him, he will give us that "defining moment," which will bring us to a point of saying with absolute assurance, "I have found my place."

CHAPTER 2

Compassion
Conceived

In my childhood home I was taught God's last name—
"Dammit," as in "God Dammit!" In that same home I was
taught that name I now hold above all others, Jesus Christ, was
to be used as an exclamation. For example, "Jesus Christ, it's
dark in here! How in the hell are we going to get out of here?"

Though I now cringe at the sound of God's name being
used that way, it was freely uttered like that in our house—
freely expressed by a four-year-old boy who was known to all
as "Danny," the second son of Vance and Maxine Nolta.

Vance Nolta and Mildred Maxine Musty, both graduates of
Central Point High School in southern Oregon, married and
made three boys together: Bill, Danny, and Mike.

Our mother was the second-to-youngest of seven children—Mom and Pop's (as we called our grandmother and
grandfather) children. A beautiful young woman of raven hair
and lithe figure, our momma reached her maturity about the
time the German armies were amassing to plunge the world
into World War II.

Our dad, Vance, the youngest son of George and Zona
Nolta, was a handsome young man with curly black hair. By
the time Mom and Dad married, two of Vance's brothers, who

would become pioneers in the agricultural aviation industry in California, were already off flying. (Dad would later join them in that industry and do pioneer flying of his own as the first pilot to fly over a forest fire and drop retardant from the air.)

My older brother, Bill, who was fair-skinned, covered in freckles, and had coal black hair, took after Pop—Bill Musty, our grandfather. Pop's ancestry was somewhere in France. Now home was Central Point, with its lumber mills and wigwam burners. Out on the north edge of town sat the creamery where Pop made butter so he could provide for Sally, his beloved wife, with whom he shared the then-obligatory "till death do us part" vow. (They made it for more than fifty years.)

After Bill, came Danny and then Michael Dean ("with a head like a bean"). We called him "licker lips," among other things. We sometimes picked on him, as big brothers will do— as my big brother, Bill, did to me. I look back on that kid-to-kid cruelty now with feelings of shame and wonder. How could I have done that to him? Could it be that I had simply learned it from those who said and did the same things to me?

I see the picture in my mind to this day: three rag-tag little boys, each in their patched jeans, standing in the dirt of the road beside the old metal-framed wire gate. Bill, as always, squinted into the midday sun as he held my hand, while I held Mikey's. We stood for that picture with our grandmother— "Mom" of the Mom and Pop duo—who patched our jeans, darned our socks, made us cookies, canned us peaches, wet our hair and slicked it down, gave us spit baths to get the ice cream off our faces, sometimes put us to bed, laughed and joked with us, hummed tunes to us, and always, *always* loved us.

Today, Mike and I share a deep love for each other, and we hurt together at the early death of our big brother, Bill. His untimely death left us with an unfilled hole in our lives. We still miss the brother who left home before he graduated high school, joined the Navy, traveled the world (seldom hitting the "home port"), retired after 22 years in El Centro, California, and then...just died. Dead at fifty-one, leaving his own little family (he had become a husband and father) and his two brothers, who really only remembered him as the "pain in the rear" he was when he left home at eighteen. Not until Bill's funeral at the Navy Air Base, where he had retired, did we come to know our big brother as others knew him—loved, competent, and friendly.

After Mom and Dad had married and started their family, they began a seemingly endless series of moves, the earliest of which (at least in my recollection) was to the tiny town of Tiller, Oregon. Dad moved us there on a pipe dream of being a logger. In my now sixty-plus-year-old mind, I can see Dad and me standing in a run-down, dusty truck tire shop that sits beside an even dustier road running through Tiller. Just down that road, jutting out over the Umpqua River, sat the tiny house Daddy moved his family into. By then there were three of us little boys. Mike was just a baby, always held or in his crib or playpen, to keep him off the dusty, splintery floors. One day a snake made its way into the house. Mom had seen enough, and we moved again. A short time later, the house fell into the river.

Moving Again...and Again

From Tiller, we moved to Colusa, California. Why Colusa? Today there is no answer to that question...just Colusa. Colusa of the 1940s was a little mosquito-infested town on the banks of the Sacramento River. My memories of Colusa are very limited, and what memories I have of the place are all bad. I remember as a young child riding my tricycle down the sidewalk when two neighborhood girls stopped me. One held my trike's handlebars while the other grabbed handfuls of sand to put in my hair. I still remember the washtubs on the back porch where Momma gave me a bath. Eventually, the house burned and we moved again.

Does it matter *where* we moved? Does it matter *why* we moved? Does it matter *how often* we moved? This little boy only knew that we moved and that each move brought pain and a "disconnect."

From Colusa, we moved to Willows, California, which was the center of the burgeoning rice-farming industry. In my mind, this was the settled, declared new home of the Noltas. But it didn't last. The war descended, and many American men—including husbands and fathers—were called away to serve their country. Among those many men was Vance Nolta, my father.

There are many stories of women left alone with children at that time. Our story hardly seems unusual, let alone spectacular. Our mother and our Nanny (as we called our mother's older sister) together moved into the house across the tracks. Now there was Mommy, us three boys, Nanny, and Cousin Sally. Nanny worked, Mommy took care of us kids, and they struggled to make ends meet. They tried as hard as they could, but they couldn't do it.

So we moved again.

Fortunately for all of us, Pop saved the day. My grandfather converted (almost miraculously, I'd say) the woodshed behind his home in Central Point into a two-room apartment for Mom and us three boys. Of those days my memory now comes sharply into focus.

I was just too young to understand what being poor meant—the poverty, the patched jeans, and the rationing. Besides, it was the only life I knew.

Standing on a stool up at the kitchen sink brushing my teeth, I could always hear the first bell ringing at Central Point Elementary. The first bell meant you had to run to get there before the second bell or you would be late for Mrs. Richardson's first grade class. Only "The Twins," the local preacher's kids, were ever late. In fact, they were *always* late.

My dad was gone. My dad, like all those other dads, was off fighting in the conflict that gripped the entire world at that time. I was sure he was a war hero. After all, he was gone, so he *had* to be a hero. And then he came home...and then he was not a hero anymore. He was just Daddy.

And again, we moved, Daddy going on ahead.

I remember that adventuresome train ride all the way from Central Point, Oregon, back to Willows, California. All sorts of thoughts about what life would be like once we got there filled my little head:

I can't wait to get off this train.

I can't wait to see Daddy again.

Daddy will take us to our house—a real house!

We will be family again.

The nightlong train ride south finally ended in Willows, home of the Willows High Honkers, named for the geese that populated the area each winter. As the train arrived in the still-sleeping little town, I realized something.

Daddy wasn't there. Where was he?

My Family and "the Bottle"

My mother's memory is better than my own, but I can still picture our trudge through the sleepy streets of Willows, California: Bill and I dragging what we could manage and Mommy carrying both a suitcase and little brother Mikey.

I loved my dad. I love him to this day, even though he has been gone since 1965. My daddy wasn't there then, and he isn't here now, and it is his fault. It was his fault then, and it is his fault now—his fault because his lifestyle and addictions cut his life way too short.

Was it Grandfather Nolta, the rough-and-tumble horse trader, who started it all? Did he infect his sons with the disease? Did he teach his sons of the pleasure, of the escape, of the bottle? Or was it just the time of war that encouraged men to take part in the "manly" exercise of standing at Fred Rabbit's outdoor bar in Willows, California, and drinking Lucky Lager beer and smoking Lucky Strike cigarettes? Was it disease, predisposition, recklessness, manliness, or just the times?

You know, it really doesn't matter. Daddy drank too much. He wasn't there, and his wife and sons suffered the pain.

Alcoholism—the ever-present squared-off bottle of Jim Beam, the ever-present bottles of beer, the ever-present family conflict over the "elephant in the front room"—became the norm in the Nolta family. The norm was that Daddy wasn't home. The norm was not enough money. The norm was the conflict between a Mommy who was trying to take care of three little boys in a too-small house while being married to a too-irresponsible husband who was too addicted to the bottle to know, to care, or to change.

And so, the fights.

My greatest pain came as I lay awake at night hearing Mommy and Daddy raising their voices. No covers, no matter how thick they were, pulled over my little head could shut out the sounds of the two people I loved most *not* loving each other. No words of consolation from Mommy following the sounds of the screeching tires of Daddy's exit could change what I had just heard.

My mind was filled constantly, not just with the uncertainties of my family situation but also with thoughts of what I could do to make things better:

What will happen to us? Will Daddy go away for good? Will there be a home for us tomorrow? Why is Mommy crying again? How can I make her stop crying? How will I be able to take care of my Mommy? From now on, I will be a good boy. I won't be naughty like Bill is...not fool around like Mike does. I will get good grades in school, keep my part of the room clean, sweep the floor, make her laugh, and always mind. I will make Mommy happy.

Let's "Pretend"

I was only seven years old, and I couldn't stop the hurt. We never had enough money, Daddy was gone too often, and Mommy was unhappy. So my brothers and I did our best to escape. We didn't "escape" like our daddy had (through the bottle), but we certainly escaped.

"Let's play a game!" one of us suggested. "Pretend we are rich kids who don't have any mom or dad. We have our own icebox full of pop, and we can have one anytime we want....I will get on my horse and ride out to get the cows. Or I'll go on my new Schwinn bike—the one with the mud flaps, horn, and a headlight on the front—and ride all over Willows as long as I want....Pretend that Dad owns a candy store, and we can take all the candy bars we want to school....Pretend that all the kids at school like us....Pretend...."

Always pretending. Is that like drinking? Is that like staying away from home when home does not have enough money and the boys are beginning to understand what is really going on? It is easier staying away from home when your wife is unhappy, easier to let Jim Beam or Lucky Lager tell you it's OK...that *you're* OK.

I was eight years old and already facing a tough life. But it was about to get worse.

When My World Came Apart

The Smiths lived next door to us, and for reasons I didn't fully understand, they fought too. Harmon Smith bullied us, and Bill wouldn't stand up to him. "Aw, Smitty's a good guy," Bill would say. Marilyn Smith was Mikey's age and Claradelle Smith was my age and a classmate of mine in Mrs. Adams's third grade class.

I liked Claradelle, but I remember vividly how one day she dropped on me the worst news I could have heard. As bad as things often were at home, my little eight-year-old mind was not prepared—could not have been prepared—for the worst news a child can hear.

A game of hopscotch was in full progress on the sidewalk when Claradelle dropped the little bomb that exploded my world, sending pieces flying off down Plumas Street.

"Your parents are getting a divorce."

Everything in front of my eyes disappeared in a flood of tears and bewilderment. Questions, fear, and panic overwhelmed my mind as I tried to comprehend—as well as an eight-year-old can—this terrible news.

Can this earthshaking news mean anything else but that Daddy will be gone from my life forever? Where can I go to stop the pain? Who can answer my questions and see me through the pain?

Only one answer came to my mind: Mommy!

"Danny, what's wrong?" my mother asked me as I ran to her in tears. "Why are you crying?"

I told her what I had learned that day, but as hard as my mother tried to ease the pain (mostly by minimizing what the news of my parents' divorce meant to me) her words of consolation were hardly comforting or consoling.

"It only means that your dad won't be staying here with us," she told me. "You will still get to see him."

I was not convinced. In my mind, divorce meant *forever*. Divorce meant you were a weirdo because it was 1947, and nobody's parents got a divorce. As far as I knew, I was the only one.

Suddenly, any hope I had of being one of the "regular" kids, of being somebody—anybody—was gone. A little hole came into my life and it slowly burned bigger. It got bigger every time someone mentioned divorce, bigger every time someone mentioned my dad, bigger every time he did not show up to see us, and bigger whenever we went to see him at the run-down hotel where he had a room.

Oh, how I loved Daddy. The drinking didn't matter to me. He was still my hero. My mother and my aunts didn't see him that way, but in my mind he was the greatest. I imagined him to be what he was not, just because I didn't want to be weird, didn't want to be a nobody.

When your dad is a mechanic he has to be the very best, as far as you're concerned. *He can fix anything*, you think. *Being a mechanic is very important.* When I stood up to the rail at Fred Rabbit's, my dad drinking his beer and me my orange soda, nothing else mattered because I was with my dad! I was somebody, especially when we were having a beer with the guys. *My dad has lots of friends,* I imagined.

But all of the imagining in the world does not fill up the hole that slowly burns bigger inside you. Little boys like I was can't understand the burning and what it means. I didn't know why it hurt, and I didn't know that when the fire finally went out I would have to fill that gaping hole so I could be something to somebody.

Oh, God, I am only eight years old. I love Mommy and Daddy, but they don't love each other anymore. It hurts so bad. No one knows how bad this hurts. Please don't make me do this by myself. It hurts too much. I'm scared. Is there someone who can be with me when it hurts in the night?

Compassion was conceived in Willows, California, during a family fight, during a hopscotch game, during times I spent standing with my dad at the rail at Fred Rabbit's. In my young mind, I could never have understood nor foreseen how God was so purposefully allowing—and using—the circumstances of my life to plant a tiny seed that would, under the gentle hands and watchful care of his servants, flower into a wonderful gift of compassion.

In the years that followed, God used every painful moment and every lonely, scary night as water and plant food to nurture this seedling of compassion to maturity and beauty.

CHAPTER 3

When I Learned God's
Real Name

Anniversary Sunday of 1956 at Medford Friends Church had been a long and busy day; now it was time for the evening service. I could hold out no longer. The currents of my life had—at first gently and then with more and more insistence and strength—brought me to the whirlpool that had been spinning at that place down the river of my life.

During the past several months of my attendance at Medford Friends I came to realize there was a whirlpool that could draw me into a new world, completely and fully. And now I was at the very edge of the spinning vortex. If I did not quickly swim away I would be pulled under.

But why would I want to swim away? Behind me were years of pain, loneliness, and emptiness. Ahead I could see love, acceptance, and forgiveness. So with open arms and a ready spirit, I was about to yield myself to the currents. It took the words and finally the invitation of Ed Harmon, a visiting pastor from Ashland Friends Church, to bring me to a point of yielding and allowing myself to be pulled in. That anniversary evening, I allowed God's Spirit entrance into my life.

After seventeen years, I was finally home. And in that home, God's last name was not "Dammit."

A Seed Planted

It had been a long seventeen years—filled with moves, suffering, isolation, confusion, and thoughts in my head no boy should have to think. Many people along the way must receive credit for getting me to the point of my conversion, but it all began with my brother Mikey. Mikey, on one windy day in our little backyard in Willows, California, gave me that first little nudge into the currents of the spiritual river of life. Today, he likely would not advise me the same way, but knowing him as well as I do, I believe he would probably say, "If that's what does it for you, go for it."

I still remember the wind blowing the limbs of the huge black walnut trees as we two little boys, one about six and the other eight, stood together in our loneliness and confusion. Out of the blue, or perhaps out of the separation he and I were feeling because Daddy was gone, Mikey said to me, "We ought to go to church."

But why would I remember that? Was it because it was so unusual, so unexpected, so "not us"? It could be all of the above, but it still sticks in my mind...not in Mikey's but certainly in mine.

The words were spoken into the air and were carried away by the northern California winds, but not before they penetrated my heart, not before God picked them up as they echoed in my inner being. From that echoed call, God responded— responded with his people, his messengers, his angels.

The message carried on the winds that day reached the ears of Mrs. Earhart, my second grade teacher at Willows Elementary, who was also a Sunday school teacher at Willows First Baptist Church. In those days teachers could ask children to go to church with them. She went to church; then I went too. I went just once, but that first memory of being in a church is significant to me to this day.

A "New" Family

A couple of years after my parents divorced, Mom remarried, and I had a stepfather, Harold. He was older than my mother and a man of some means in that little town. He owned a car dealership and employed several men, among them, at one time, my father and my Uncle Loyal. Harold was the kind of man every boy dreams of knowing. He drove fine cars, had a pop machine that was always full, and provided the coveted bologna and cheese for the sandwiches that previously were often mayo and mustard because there was nothing else to go between the pieces of bread.

With Harold came Roger and Don, his two sons. By that time, they were college-bound big brothers. They never seemed to compete with us but rather to gather us in, share their dad with us, take us to visit college, and always protect us around their friends when it came to "big-boy talk." Don would always caution his friends, "Careful! Little ears!"

With Harold also came alcohol. At every event, every holiday, every trip to visit people, every visit by people to our house—Harold would offer this invitation: "How about a drink?"

Another father, but more alcohol and all that came with it. There were more arguments in the night, more ducking under the covers, more screeching of tires, more holes in my life, more doubts of my worth, and more loneliness.

Two years later, in 1950, our world of pop when we wanted it, new cars to ride in, bologna and cheese for our sandwiches, and well-being all came to an end. Chrysler Motors workers went on strike, and they produced no new cars for months. My dealership-owning stepfather went from prosperity to poverty, and we moved. It was never the same again.

We went from job to job and from house to house. From Willows back to Central Point for a short few months that are today a blur, and then to Paradise, California, where we lived in three different houses in a year—always moving in a hurry.

In Paradise, God sent another of his messengers. This time it was not sweet Mrs. Earhart; it was crabby Mrs. Boles, my sixth grade teacher. Though a stern and strict disciplinarian, Mrs. Boles each day took out a worn King James Bible and read to us. Those were foreign words to me. I still don't remember much of anything she read, but somehow she instilled in me the importance of that Book and laid some groundwork for those who would later influence my life.

From Paradise, we moved to Chico—another move, another house, another angel messenger. Rodney Tull, who lived in the next block, was my friend in the midst of my eighth grade year. Genuine Levi's, fluorescent-colored stocking caps, and real Converse tennis shoes were all "in," but we couldn't afford any of them. Girls were in also, but the only girl I could get up the courage to ask to the school dance was Nancy, who sat in front of me in eighth grade home room. Nancy, a nice girl, had a haircut that made her look like the Nancy in the "Sluggo" comic strip—definitely not the one I wanted to take to the eighth grade dance.

Rodney, angel of God, to the rescue.

Rodney had a paper route; I rode my bike with him and helped. He was a happy guy. He went to church and I went with him. My young mind questioned, "What is this stuff all about? Why am I embarrassed that other families go to church and ours doesn't? Why do I feel left out when they pray at the church party? Why don't I feel comfortable or 'fit in'?"

Another seed planted, but it was a foreign seed because in my house God's last name was still Dammit.

In Chico my half-sister Sue Anne was born. All of us welcomed this darling little girl. She was destined to be spoiled, doted on, and idolized by all of us. (According to her, however, none of that happened.)

Also in Chico the "settledness"—if you want to call it that—of the alcoholic family became apparent. Bill, an accomplished shoplifter for the past several years, was now our "family felon." He was arrested for shoplifting, put in juvenile hall, and became an embarrassment to our mother. Mikey continued his fooling around, joking his way through life and playing it out as best he could. I never asked him how he felt about anything. Other than the fact that he was the family clown, he is gone from my memories of those years.

I became the family rescuer. I tried hard in school, poured oil on the waters of the family, and made sure I wasn't like Bill or Mike. It is funny now that I think about it, because they were doing the same thing—making sure they were not like Danny. The patterns were well established—a rebel, a rescuer, and a clown. By my eighth grade year, the patterns of my life were firmly set.

Trying to "Fit In"

From Chico we moved back "home" to Central Point, Oregon. With eighth grade behind me and high school looming, things got tougher for me. Now I was a little boy playing with the big boys, and I could do nothing to change that fact.

I eagerly answered the Charles Atlas ad, the one that promises you a muscular, strong body. *Now the bully would not kick sand in my face. Now I could have big muscles and be able to compete with the other boys, play sports, and have a girlfriend who didn't look like Nancy. Now I could finally be somebody.* But the Charles Atlas response I received in the mail only asked for money to buy the *real* program, the one I could put into practice to look like the guys in the pictures—the guys with bulging muscles and handsome faces—the ones to be reckoned with. But we were broke and I was little. If people had asked me if I was a ninety-eight-pound weakling, I would have had to honestly say, "Not yet!" The big guys would pick me up and carry me down the hall, laughing the whole time.

The hole in my life only got bigger.

My freshman year at Crater High School I was a Crater Comet. Black and white crepe paper decorated the halls and the smell of football was in the air. In football, there are only the quick or the dead. I was not quick and I didn't want to be dead, so I passed up football, instead envying all those big, quick guys.

Basketball follows football. Five-foot-one hardly qualified me to make the freshman boys' basketball team, but I had to try. Somehow, I had to be one of the guys, had to be somebody, and this must be the way. I wanted to be one of the "jocks" so people would know that Danny Nolta, the son of a broke mechanic, was somebody other than the little guy they laughed at and carried down the hall.

And so I turned out. I raced up and down the floor for two weeks, feebly shot baskets, got a bad case of the shin splints, and failed to impress Coach Knapp. He cut me off the freshman boys' basketball team. I was crushed.

Coach Knapp, however, was an angel in disguise. As I gathered my stuff and prepared to vacate the locker room, this ex-Marine who was now the Crater High P.E. teacher as well as the track coach and frosh basketball coach, sprouted angel wings. He asked, "Would you like to be the freshman boys basketball team statistician?"

At that moment, I didn't even know what a statistician was, but I found out that he kept records of each game. For me, though, it really meant sublimation—channeling my need to "be somebody" in a different direction. I may not have known what the word *statistician* meant, but I quickly came to know what it *felt* like to be one. It felt like I had found something to fill that all-consuming hole of neediness. It was not what I *wanted* to put into it, but like a gnawing hungry stomach that is full on porridge or full on fillet mignon, it does not care, because it is full.

I have since learned that, really, love and sublimation make the world go around. By taking the proffered job, I could be a part of the team. I could travel with the team and be *needed* by the team. *Coach Knapp needs me! The team needs me! Oh, it's not running up and down the floor being a hero, but they need me! They need Danny Nolta! I'll do it, Coach Knapp! I will be the best statistician you have ever had!*

I wasn't a *big* somebody, but I was somebody. I was the statistician. Season followed season, and with Coach Knapp's encouragement I became team manager for all of the teams he assisted with. Team manager—team go-fer. I was a part of something! "Danny, do this, Danny do that. Could you? Would you?" They needed me!

I had found my way. My energy, my drive to be some-body—anybody—could be satisfied by "doing" for people. They would need me, and I would feel important and needed. Danny Nolta had found a place at Crater High School, but, more importantly, he had found a place in life. There was a place to stand, to be recognized, to fit in, to *be*.

More Seeds of Faith

Somewhere along the river of life, I met the Smith twins, Gary and Larry. I don't remember exactly how or when I met them.

It was probably when we moved back to Central Point that last time, when I was in eighth grade. They lived right down Seventh Street from me, across from the park. They were handsome, smart...and different.

I found out how different Gary and Larry Smith were the first time I was in their house. I saw Bibles and pictures of Jesus. They prayed before meals, went to church. And they made no bones about any of it. The more I hung around the twins, the more I admired their family. But I also became more embarrassed about the differences between their family and mine. Not so with them, however. They were never judgmental and never put me down. They were always nice to my mom and never "preachy."

It was at the Smith twins' house that I first met the man who became my spiritual mentor. I was having dinner there one evening when their preacher, Clynton Crisman, came calling.

"Clynton, good to see you!" came the greeting. "Do you want to have dinner with us?"

"Sure, why not," he accepted, and sat down across the table from me. This was as close as I had ever been to a real live preacher, and I survived. Little did I know that there was a "God-type conspiracy" going on that evening.

My sophomore-year biology teacher, Mr. Sutherland, lived just a block or two down the street from me. He was my favorite teacher, and he had a big old picture of Jesus in his living room. He was also one of the advisors for a Boy Scout Explorer post that a number of us boys joined—not for merit badges but for the opportunity to go camping, which we did, lots.

At one of our meetings they announced: "Next Sunday is Boy Scout Sunday, and you boys need to make sure you go to church." As good Scouts, we were to follow the directives of our advisors. The problem? None of us went to church anywhere. So what would we do? It was unanimous: "Let's all go to the Smith twins' church." That Sunday morning, the Smith family picked up Jerry Kime and me and transported us to Medford Friends Church. "This isn't too bad," we said. "But hey, Bayard Stone is not here. He lives just down the street. Let's go get him." And we did.

A Place to Really "Fit In"

From the moment I hit the door of the church, I didn't want to escape where the currents of my life had delivered me. I was shocked, stunned, overwhelmed, surprised...and delighted. I didn't know Adam from Moses, and I didn't know how to sing from a hymnal or know my way around. But I did know this: From the very instant I arrived at church, I knew I was loved and accepted. So I stayed.

I went to church three Sundays in a row, and my brothers started calling me the "white sheep" of the family. Honestly, though, I was beyond caring what my family thought or what others might say about me. I had found the group of adults I was looking for, and I had also found a group of kids in the Christian Endeavor youth program who accepted me, encouraged me, didn't make fun of me, and took me for who I was. They genuinely wanted me to be a part of them.

Over the next couple of months I got to be a regular at Medford Friends. I didn't understand what was going on, but I knew I liked it. And then I went away—off to California to live with my dad, stepmother, and two stepbrothers. That summer I worked on the loading crew as my dad flew for his brothers, who owned Willows Flying Service. I also wrote to a blue-eyed blonde who was the Medford Friends youth group's secret weapon in getting boys to come be a part of the group. I was "in love" and chomping at the bit to get back to Medford and my steady girlfriend...even if our "romance" had been by mail.

Summer ended, and on my very first evening back home, Jerry Kime and Bayard Stone picked me up and took me to a Crater High Sportsman's Club party. As soon as I got in the car with my two best friends I resumed the normal language (swearing) that had always been a part of my life. But Bayard looked at me and quietly said, "We don't talk like that any more. We are Christians now."

What happened to my two friends? We had tried any number of times to give up that kind of language, even having contests to see who could keep from swearing the longest, which I always lost. All I could think to say to Bayard was, "OK."

My second big surprise of the evening was my friends' innocent announcement that the blue-eyed blonde, Medford Friends Church's secret weapon of male youth evangelism, had been dating another friend of ours all summer. In fact, they were going steady.

My two best friends' newfound faith was perhaps the final push I needed as I sped toward the place and time of my surrender to the God who had loved me all of my seventeen years. He had birthed me to my very own mom and dad and had used every circumstance of my life to bring me to this moment. Now I was at the edge of the whirlpool, swimming as fast as I could to that moment of immersion.

With my conversion that night came a new sense of freedom and a new joy. That night I drove my Model A Ford (an antique car by 1956) home and sang at the top of my lungs, "This world is not my home. I'm just a passing through...."

A Different— *Very* Different—Kind of Family

At Medford Friends Church I was surrounded by loving people. Among them were Pastor Crisman, who would later be my role model for pastoring, and his wife, Marjorie. Marj taught our high school class, and we all loved her. Dr. Wayne and Bertie Roberts were a part of the Roberts clan that formed a significant part of the congregation. They became my "other" parents, encouraging me and loving me every step of the way.

When it came time for college, I had a problem: I just couldn't financially afford to go. But I received a letter saying that an anonymous donor had put money in my account, enabling me to attend George Fox College in Newberg, Oregon. Only years later did I learn that it was Dr. Wayne and Bertie who had paid my way.

Through the constant love, encouragement, and nurturing of my brothers and sisters at Medford Friends, I grew spiritually and emotionally. I also began to progress toward a time and place of healing.

And it wasn't long before they were saying to me, "Dan, we believe God is calling you to be a pastor."

CHAPTER 4

Compassion: Evidence of Personal Healing

New Christians who enter into pastoral ministry without understanding deeply who they are in Christ and how the kingdom of God works often pay the price with daytime furrowed brows and sleepless nights trying to figure out how they fit into God's workaday kingdom.

I had been a pastor for several years before I read the book that turned on within me the lights of understanding about how the kingdom works. It was E. Stanley Jones's *Is the Kingdom of God Realism?*

While that book gave me much of the understanding I needed, I still questioned how *I* personally fit into a place of service in God's kingdom. Struggling to keep up intellectually, and dealing with my chaotic past with all of the emotional wounds barely scabbed over, I was left wondering.

Another book came to the rescue.

I don't remember exactly how Henri Nouwen's book got into my hands; but it did. I had never heard of the author but I found the title, *The Wounded Healer*, intriguing. Its analysis of ministry in a contemporary society interested me. Not until I reached the title chapter of the book did my heart begin to respond and say, "This is about me. *I* am a wounded healer."

Here is a short excerpt from that chapter:

> He is called to be the wounded healer, the one who must look after his own wounds but at the same time be prepared to heal the wounds of others...but also to make his wounds into a major source of his healing power...but what are our wounds?...loneliness best expresses our immediate experience and therefore most fittingly enables us to understand our brokenness.

I had never questioned the existence of wounds in my own life. They were most certainly there. For me, the question was what else to do about them besides what I had already done—forgiving those who had delivered the blows. The pain would still occasionally "wake me" or "jab at me" in times of stress, causing me to revert to the mechanisms I had long ago devised to deal with it—mostly working extra hard to be approved. That often caused me to fall over exhausted, weeping out to the Lord in the words of a classic hymn, "Nothing in my hand I bring...only to Thy cross I cling."

Nouwen's book answered so many questions and liberated me to be who I am: a "wounded healer." I could now actually use the very wounds that caused so much pain. They were for me a university education in the understanding of those I was drawn to and sought out: the other "woundeds" who surrounded me.

If the words of Henri Nouwen were my own autobiography, there would be much yet to be written. I would write of my college years, the birth of my half-brother Scott, my marriage to Judi and our raising of our five natural children and three foster children, my entrance to pastoral ministry, and my years as a police chaplain. But the autobiography to the time of my conversion simply sets the stage for the development of a compassionate spirit that began by nurture and was completed in the process of conversion.

Choosing Healing, Choosing Forgiveness

If I professed to have things fully figured out or if I were to say, even at this time in my life, that I am all healed and completely well, you would know by the writing that it is not so. I can only profess that I have forgiven those who injured me so long ago—those like my dad, who learned how to be a father from the only father he had.

I have chosen to forgive as I have been forgiven. I have chosen—in the vein of Charlie Plumb, a fighter pilot in the Vietnam War who was taken captive and held in the "Hanoi Hilton" for six years and tortured daily—to be "better, not bitter."

The evidence of the compassionate spirit God has given me has convinced me of his healing power, which began a work in me at my conversion and continues to this day. My willingness to follow the Lord's call to become a pastor and later a police chaplain convinced me that his healing work was being accomplished and that he wanted to put it to good use for the benefit of others.

I have chosen to "allow" God to have dragged me through it all that he might shape me into exactly what he wants me to be. And if that required my being wounded, then I glory in the wounds. Those very wounds have been enablers and door openers. They have provided for me glimpses of light into the souls of those I have been privileged to walk with through their pain. I have been able to stand beside them without causing further pain or embarrassment because I have experienced the wounds, pain, and embarrassment myself.

Learning to "Enter In"

This writing is not from an academic background, for I have often mentally fought with academia over maintaining distance and objectivity when seeking to help another in crisis. It always seemed to be the antithesis of who I was. The thoughts of Henri Nouwen in *The Wounded Healer* were much more in line with the way I felt and more congruent with the way it has worked for me—and can work for others in the "helping" professions. I came to answer Nouwen's rhetorical question as he did when he wrote, "Who can take away suffering without entering into it?" The answer? "No one!"

The question is always, "Nature or nurture?" In other words, does God simply *give* you the gift you need to be useful in his kingdom? With God, nothing is wasted—neither the good times nor bad times, neither the pain nor the privilege. In my mind, it is not possible that I endured such terrible pain for naught, not possible that it was used *just* to drive me to my knees. I did not suffer it only to have it set aside as if nothing had happened. No life experience is a throwaway with God. He ultimately used the experiences, the wounds, the pain, and the suffering creatively to shape my personality, and more importantly, to convert me to my giftedness.

Those wounds of life—the wounds such as insecurity, fear, loneliness, and a depreciated self-worth that came from an alcoholic, absent father—shaped the young man who met God at Medford Friends. With conversion of my soul came the beginning of the healing/conversion of my mind and emotions. In that healing process God did not simply throw away all that happened but instead applied this wonderful promise: "And we know that in all things God works for the good of those who love him, who have been called according to his pur-pose" (Romans 8:28).

God took the bad things—every drink of Jim Beam, every family fight, every moment of fear and insecurity, every mo-ment of little-boy suffering, and every wound of the heart—and created out of them a compassionate spirit that was now will-ing, but not quite ready, to be used of him.

It is now also apparent to me that from the psychological mechanisms I had created in my life to survive, to achieve, and to be somebody, God began crafting for me the gift that so fits the wounded spirit: the gift of compassion. God did not dis-count or overlook the wounds; he instead used them to my benefit. Instead of counseling me, "Forget it; let the past be the past," he used the past to help create the present and to give me the gift.

Compassion is the gift that "suffers with," the gift that wills us to walk alongside and enter into the pain, suffering, and woundedness of another. It is the gift that wills us to run to-ward the one in pain while others run away. It is the gift that bids us rescue with an others-centered, not self-centered atti-tude.

While my own insecurity was self-centered, God's gift of compassion allowed me to focus on the needs of others—not just to be needed, not just to be liked, but instead just to genu-inely act out of love.

In short, I had experienced love, and now I wanted to share love.

A Bountiful Reciprocity

The apostle Paul wrote, "Praise be to the God and Father of our Lord Jesus Christ, the Father of compassion and the God of all comfort, who comforts us in all our troubles, so that we can comfort those in any trouble with the comfort we ourselves have received from God" (2 Corinthians 1:3-4).

I had received comfort, and now I wanted to give comfort. Indeed, my own need for comforting, now satisfied, equipped me to give it to others. I could rejoice in my woundedness because it now had a purpose: the comfort of others. As Paul goes on to say, "For just as the sufferings of Christ flow over into our lives, so also through Christ our comfort overflows. If we are distressed, it is for your comfort and salvation..." (2 Corinthians. 1:5-6).

In the workings of his kingdom, God has supplied a bountiful reciprocity, demonstrated in the gift of compassion. I have joyously discovered that as I meet the needs of others, my own needs are met. For example, in my own loneliness I have sought out others similarly lonely, and we have found companionship.

My own wounds have caused this sense of loneliness; I think: *No one understands, no one is like me, I stand alone.* People who are in their own crisis or who are suffering the effects of tragedy or trauma are similarly affected. They express a sense of uniqueness, a sense of abandonment. They feel as though they are alone in their tragedy and may think or say things such as, "This is happening to me, and no one else understands."

Fortunately for the suffering, there are those gifted with compassion, those who are willing to intervene. They are most often the ones who have suffered loneliness or abandonment themselves and who are not willing that another should suffer alone. In exercising this gift, the compassionate one comes alongside the victim and meets his or her needs. In that, the victim's need for another to walk with him or her is met and the long-term effects of the crisis are mitigated.

Christian psychologist H. Norman Wright, in a lecture I heard, stated the qualities of those who survived a crisis. The first he listed is, "They had one person who stood with them." That one person may meet the need for companionship and take away the sense of abandonment that so many victims of crisis feel acutely. In cases like that, the exercise of the gift of compassion meets the needs of both in a legitimate and helpful way.

Kinship out of Crisis

After almost all of the thousands of crisis responses I've done over thirty-plus years, I would return home feeling I had "made contact" with another human being, and at the worst moment of his or her life. For me, it became far more than a crisis contact; it became a kinship contact. There was another brother or another sister with whom I could share a little piece of life. That seeking of connectedness motivates the compassionate person to exercise the most-needed gift.

On a dark night, ones who have felt that deeply rooted sense of loneliness, arise from their beds in response to a dispatcher's call. They go to meet one whose crisis circumstance has brought such an immediate and profound sense of aloneness that he or she willingly accepts a stranger as an intimate companion to share the pain.

In August 1988 I wrote Bobby & Me

Dear Friends across America:

"Are you allowed to go in there?" were the words from the mouth of four-year-old little Bobby as we stood outside the TAC (short for Tactical) van last night. *What's a four-year-old doing up at that time of night? What was I doing up at that time of night?* Both of us would rather have been in bed, but somehow we were "partners" together as we waited—waited for Bobby's mom to give her statement to the detective *and* for his dad to give it up and come out of the apartment.

An alcoholic binge had put Bobby's dad "over the edge." Threats of Bobby's life and a shot fired from the 9mm automatic had finally driven his mom from the apartment...a few hours later we were buddies, waiting for the outcome.

I had watched this bright little guy, number 81 (his t-shirt said so), go through chocolate milk, toast, and two popsicles at the neighbor's as the evening wore on. Now he was restless. "What will happen to my dad?" was his unspoken question. If he had asked, I could not have answered. I had questions too. *Will he shoot himself? Will he come out shooting and force us into a shoot-back situation? Will he just walk out?*

Bobby and I had played ball in the neighbor's living room; tickled, talked, and built some trust. Now we just waited. I watched his seemingly unending energy finally begin to run out as he twisted, jumped, ran, and chattered outside the van. In the warmth of the summer night, my mind focused on Bobby.

Bobby, who are you? Do you have any idea what might happen tonight that could so drastically alter your life? What will happen to you? Will you one day turn to alcohol and be as sick emotionally and spiritually as your dad? Will you too, one day, be "holding the cops off"?

By 2 a.m. it was over and I was on my way home. No big deal! A little sobering up, accompanied by some light tear gas, and Bobby's dad was on his way to jail, safe and sound. But it isn't really over, is it?

There are still the questions about Bobby's future. Until the future answers them, it will have to be enough for him to remember that one warm summer's evening, a guy called chaplain, wearing a cop's jacket, played ball with him, hugged him and waited with him—for reasons "little number 81" didn't even understand.

◇

At this writing, Bobby, if he is still living, is twenty-four years old—old enough to be a rebel, a rescuer, or a clown. My desire for him today is this: "Oh little Bobby, use the fear, hurt, and loneliness of that night to produce in you compassion for others. I pray to God that you are this day standing with others in their moments of pain."

Converted for a Purpose

God's conversion is complete and thorough—including body, mind, and spirit. In my case, he brought understanding of all the mechanisms I had created to feel worthwhile—mechanisms such as my busyness—and converted them to his purposes. He has given me the realization that I do not need to be busy to be worthwhile but can be worthwhile simply because he loves me and deems me so. *Busy* was no longer the end of all but rather the means to accomplish what God had laid out for me to do for his kingdom.

The living presence of Christ, the truly compassionate One, converts insecurity, which demands action (and only causes us to compete), and "doing," which so many of us have long equated with worth, into compassionate action. When we are in his presence, instead of letting our fears and doubts drive us (Who loves me? What am I worth?), our conversion answers those fears and doubts and gives us the correct motivation for acting.

Compassion is a precious gift to be shared with a generous, motivated spirit, the same spirit Jesus demonstrated in this verse: "When he saw the crowds he had compassion on them because they were harassed and helpless, like sheep without a shepherd" (Matthew 9:36).

Jesus' motivation was divine love, and he saw the need of those who clamored after him, those who were distressed by repeated attacks on their religion, customs, and very lives. They wandered lost, seeking their bearings and their emotional grounding. Jesus suffered with them, as he too was set upon by the religious leaders and was homeless and on a journey in a strange land away from his heavenly home. He identified with their pain and was unwilling to walk away and leave it unshared.

The one gifted with compassion likewise sees the "harassed and helpless" in crisis or caught in tragic circumstance. The compassionate one cannot help but do what Jesus did and step alongside them and proclaim, "I have been there. I know the way. Let me walk with you."

Each time I have come to one of those "aha" moments—as I did when I discovered that *The Wounded Healer* really was about me—I have had to stop and take time to reflect. Reflection always brings me back to the basics of my life journey and to the basics of being a part of the kingdom of God, and these things mesh so well.

God sought me out and drew me to himself through people who were—to me at the time, anyway—God incarnate. They taught me by example and through the Scriptures what the kingdom of God is really about. They made me desire the kingdom much like the man desired the hidden treasure in the field or the merchant who desired the pearl of great price (Matthew 13:44-45). Finally, the price was paid, but that was not the end. The King will not allow unbound, unhealed wounds on his servants. He carefully pours out the Balm of Gilead, healing the wounds. He took me, now a part of his kingdom and with fresh understanding of my wounds, and sent me out with the desire to seek out others who have been wounded.

Those very wounds—at least bound, if not completely healed—have allowed me entrance into the lives of those who suffer. But they have allowed me more than entrance. They have also allowed me an understanding and an ability to suffer with those who are suffering...to their comfort and to their healing.

Has it been worth the pain of the wounds?

Yes! A thousand times, yes.

CHAPTER 5

A Gift Given,
a Gift Received

Long before I could adequately articulate my thoughts about the gift of compassion, I understood there was a price to be paid in ministering it. At the same time, I understood that compassion was the key to effective intervention and the foundation to any ministry I would have. It was my gift to be given, and I wanted it to be received.

Over and over I gave. Over and over others received.

To talk of how I have given that gift is not so difficult—that is what this book is all about—but I find it hard to talk of those who responded to the gift and made its value known through their expressions of appreciation. That's because, in my mind anyway, talking of those who have expressed their appreciation seems boastful and denigrating of the gift itself.

Most of us recognize that from time to time our motives might be suspect—so much so that we feel the need to quickly confess those times when we feel certain others have seen right through us. Throughout my ministry I have made my confessions so that people will understand that I realize any compassion I have is a gift from God.

With that in front of me, I can also blush and feel tears welling up when I read through cards and letters from those I sought to assist. The cards bring back memories of the times I drove away from the scene of a tragedy knowing by the telltale hurt deep inside me that I had truly shared the gift of compassion. I knew because I had suffered with them.

When I have known and shared in people's suffering, cried their tears, and felt their pain and loneliness, a "thank you" card doesn't cause me to give in to pride. Rather I release tears of joy that come from knowing that the God of all compassion has used me. I know he used the deep inner loneliness and hurt inside of me, as well as his redemption, to help me identify, empathize, and, ultimately, assist another wounded, hurting soul.

A Part of a Family—a Hurting Family

Sometimes the hurting people who have come my way were so close to me that the pain I took on was almost unbearable. It was almost as if it was *my* pain and someone else had come as the compassionate one to share it. That's the way it was when I dealt with police deaths.

Police officers and those who serve with them develop a special bond, a brotherhood if you will. For more than thirty years I have been a part of that brotherhood, walking, riding, and sometimes crying with my comrades. That fact keeps memories alive—memories of notifications I did for police families when their officer sons were killed.

In September 1988 I wrote

Dear Friends across America:

It's because we are a family, I thought as I begged out of the Bible study group I was to lead. *It's because we are a family,* I thought as I quickly changed clothes and went toward the West Precinct as fast as or maybe a little faster than the law would allow.

From Prince George's, Maryland, to Tacoma, Washington, we are a family, and one of our family was even then dying.

At about 6:30 that evening I was sitting at the dining room table enjoying the dinner Judi had fixed, not even aware that the door was about to be "kicked in" on that crack house, not even aware that part of our family was in mortal danger.

Mark, a fourteen-year veteran policeman—so proud, so confident, so competent—rushed through the door first and right into the waiting volley of bullets. Only life-support systems in ICU were still "breathing" by the time our department got the call to notify Mark's mother here in Tacoma, more than 3,000 miles from his hospital room.

The message: "Your son Mark has been gravely wounded in the line of duty. He will be on life support until morning. He will not live when life support is withdrawn." Simple words but so hard to understand. Thick black clouds envelope the mind, and words and titles, like "chaplain," don't register.

Mark's mom, Mark's dad, we want so badly to have you know that even though thousands of miles separated us—different department, different uniform—it didn't matter. He was family. All of the law enforcement family shares your grief, were my thoughts.

❖

Later that month, the guy I still fondly call "boss," the then-sheriff of Pierce County, Chuck Robbins, received a card.

Note of Appreciation

Dear Sheriff Robbins:

My beloved son, Mark Kevin Murphy, a police officer in Prince George's County, Maryland, was accidentally shot and killed during a narcotics raid the evening of August 31, 1988. I received notification through your department from Chaplain Dan Nolta. The purpose of this letter is to express my sincere appreciation for the comfort and compassion I received from Chaplain Nolta. He is truly God's servant of whom you should be most proud! His prayers and understanding made a heartbreaking situation bearable.

⬦

Compassion, the gift of "suffering with," made all the difference. Nothing cold, nothing sterile, no pat answers, no clichés hastily spoken, just the gift of compassion given. It had to be enough. Nothing else applied that night or in the days to follow.

Five years later, the circumstances repeated, and again I found myself on the way to locate the parents of a "brother" who was killed in the line of duty. Among all of the death notifications I have done over the years, this one counts right up there for my most personally traumatic.

In September 1993 I wrote

Dear Ed:

Though I did not know you a few weeks ago, I know you now. I am only sorry I know you in death and did not know you in life...it is hardly fair.

A little over two hours after they ran the stop sign and smashed into your patrol car on the Los Angeles street, I was in my car going to do a job that every police chaplain dreads but holds sacred...notifying the family of a police officer killed in the line of duty.

Did it make a difference that it was 0400 in the morning, or even that you were not a part of the agency I work with? You know the answer to that, and so did your chief and so did the sergeant that requested I go. Ed, only you and I know what a privilege it was for me to go that morning and be the one who would hurt your parents so deeply and yet, hopefully, help as well.

Ed, it would have been comical if it were not so tragic, the way I tried to find your parents, who were spending the night in Seattle. I was worried that they would find out by a phone call, on the radio, or some way that no parent should hear such news. But finally it was me and them.

I am sure they taught you in the training academy that there is often time, space, and reality distortion in critical incidents. I now know that it is true...as I looked into your parents' eyes and told them there had been an accident and you had been killed. The pain was almost overwhelming as I imagined my wife and myself sitting there as the chaplain was telling us it was *our* son the cop, just about your age, who had been killed.

Ed, from that point on, every action on the part of your parents, your department, your sisters, your fiancée, and others told me about your quality of life and, beyond that, that you were loved. That demonstrated love only enhanced my feeling of what a privilege it was to serve you and your parents.

Thank you for allowing me to have a part in sharing in the pain.

May you rest in the Lord.

◇

For years after the notification and the participation in Ed's funeral that followed, I received cards from his parents giving me "Just a reminder that we have not forgotten you," as they put it. The "effectiveness" of that notification and the help that followed was my own trauma, my own suffering with them. Again, the gift was given...and received.

Routine? Anything But!

Over the years, I have responded to countless murders, suicides, and deaths of all kinds and manners, but they were not all spectacular, headline-grabbing events. There were the routine days, even those days when death notifications were made.

In March 2003 I wrote

"Just a routine death notification," is a statement that may make some of you cringe and question, "How can that be?" After so many years of doing them, they are no longer terrifying. But they do make my heart thump a bit, as I am always a little anxious. Such was the case early one morning a few weeks ago.

It was just a routine death notification to a woman whose brother had died out of state. The sheriff's department was asked to notify her. My thinking went something like this: *Hmm, an elderly brother, probably a natural death. He's older, so she will probably not be too upset...see, just a routine death notification.* Wrong again Dan! You will never forget this one.

Very shortly, I arrived at a neatly trimmed house on a quiet street in the little town of Edgewood. It was still early, so I watched for signs of life in the house. Soon, a very pleasant woman came to the door. I informed her I was from the sheriff's department, showed her my ID, and asked if I might come in. With some apprehension, she invited me in. *Oh, oh, the first snag...two little boys. Rule Number-something says you do not do notifications in front of children.*

Grandma said, "Boys, go back in the room and play." They did, and the problem was solved. That was easy. And now, "I am sorry to have to tell you...."

She took the news with a start, and then followed with the softly spoken words, "The Lord has released him. The Lord has released him." There was no anger, no questioning, and no denial. Hers were quiet words of completion, acceptance, and approval. God is good. He had delivered her eighty-four-year-old paraplegic brother from the burden of his body. Quietly, we joined hands and prayed a prayer of thanksgiving.

"And now I had better get busy and fix these boys some pancakes," she said, and followed me to the door. The early morning fog was lifting and the bright, wintry sun was beginning to filter through the bare limbs of the trees in her yard. Her words, which surely prompted this writing, have been on my heart and mind: "What a wonderful day to go to heaven."

A traumatic notification? A routine notification? Hardly. More of a soul-warming, inspiring, glad-I-get-to-do-this kind of notification. There are those moments, and I love and cherish them.

◇

As you look back and review many of the incidents in your own life, you will find that some you may have called "routine" were anything but, simply because they presented you with the opportunity to share the gift of compassion. It may be something as simple and "everyday" as a chance encounter in the supermarket aisle, where you meet a neighbor you haven't seen for some time. She tells you that her husband has cancer. You listen intently as she tells you the story then thanks you for taking time to listen. You cry with her, hug her, encourage her, and then move away from her as you pay for your groceries and go home. That special gift given and received has turned the routine into the glorious.

Someone has said that one of the personality characteristics of an emergency responder is that he or she is "internally motivated." This is equally true of those who are gifted with a compassionate spirit. It is not about money or fame or personal recognition, nor about the rush of adrenaline—as good as that can be. It is about the sheer love of humanity, a love so pure it does not demand reward other than the fulfillment of God's command to "love one another."

Who can doubt that love brought Christ to earth and took him to the cross for us? Likewise, who can doubt that love for another human being, known or unknown, is what motivates us toward compassionate acts? As he suffered for us, we suffer with them.

The one who receives the gift of compassion responds out of the knowledge that he or she has been truly loved, not with a superficial love, which demands reward, but rather with a love that reaches into the middle of the pain and takes some for itself. Compassion shares the tears. We share the grief so that we together become like Jesus, "acquainted with grief."

You have received the cards. You have felt eyes upon you that are filled at once with pain and love—the pain of the circumstances but the love for you because that person knows without a doubt that you have given of yourself in an unusual way.

Their eyes say, "You have stood beside me when I was at my worst, and loved me anyway. You have taken a part of my pain. You have been human enough to cry with me. You have been honest enough to tell me, 'There is nothing I can say,' and that was OK. I didn't need platitudes, clichés, or clever words; I needed another human being who would be courageous enough to face the awfulness with me...and you were. I needed another human being who would stand with me knowing that we could not change the unchangeable, only live through it together...and you did that."

That sums up dozens and dozens of cards and letters I have received over the years. Are they unlike yours? I think not. If you have given the gift of compassion, the gift has been received and recognized as unique among all that have ever been given.

Giving, But for What Reason?

Everything genuine has a counterfeit. For every wonderful gift, there is a perversion that impersonates and twists the original into something ugly, demeaning, and destructive.

Within each of us is the ongoing struggle to keep the gifts of God from being tarnished. We struggle to maintain the purity of that which he has given so that we might achieve the maximum for him and not for ourselves. Thus I have found it with the gift of compassion. It can be counterfeited; it can be tarnished.

As I have allowed God's Spirit to lay bare my inner self, thus exposing my *real* motives, I have had to face the fact that at times I have struggled to keep my motives pure. I have had to ask myself, "Just *why* am I doing this?"

I have found in police chaplaincy that many people struggle to keep their motives pure. I have known some (and indeed

I count myself among them at times) who get a little "puffed up" with the heady stuff of riding in cop cars and having police ID, maybe even a badge.

The same, however, can be true of anyone who associates with any organization with lines of authority and chain of command—such as a hospital or other medical facility, or even the neighborly homeowners' association. It may also be true for the one who delivers the chocolate cake to her sick neighbor, not in the true spirit of compassion, but in order to prove to all that she does, after all, hold the title of "The World's Best Baker."

I would like to believe that Mother Teresa could never have been so accused, even after she began to receive so much media attention. Those we count among the true "spiritual giants" are surely the ones who have mastered themselves through humble and moment-by-moment submission to the Spirit, who do not succumb to pride or selfishness and thus pervert this most precious gift.

For most of us, however, we can safely begin with this premise: We *can* do the right things but for the wrong reasons, the most common of which is the need to feel needed.

The Need to be Needed

Most of the time, perversion of the gift of compassion has its roots in our own neediness. It has its expression when we say "Yes" to self and "No" to the Spirit who dwells within us, when we attempt to use those unsanctified, uncommitted areas of our lives in doing good things for others.

Let's say I bake that chocolate cake, proudly frost it and decorate it with sliced almonds and delectable cherries, carry it to my neighbor, and then hope against hope that she will "ooh" and "ah" over it. Then she'll announce to all our neighbors that

I brought it and it was the best gift her household had ever received. Let's also say that she is nominating me for neighbor of the year—maybe even saint of the year!

A corny example perhaps, but it seems much safer for me than to talk about a speech I delivered to a victim panel and how I felt disappointed that I was not publicly praised for it. Much safer than telling of the times I offered assistance to a deputy and was told I was not needed, then went away smarting because I felt I had been rebuffed. In those instances, I again felt the pains of childhood and recognized the rearing of the ugly head of my nemesis: the need to be needed.

At that point the devil, the enemy of my soul, attacks: "See, you have not changed. God has not made you different. You are not a compassionate person; you only do this because you want to meet your own needs and not the needs of others."

When I recognize these attitudes and thoughts creeping in, I go to my place of retreat and get with my heavenly Father and give them to him, knowing full well that everything I am and everything I do belong to him.

Doing Versus Being

"Being" has taken a very real second place to "doing," and we are the worse for it. The lure of doing is often the undoing of a genuinely compassionate act that in the end finds its reward. In retirement, I promised myself time to work on my "being," which has too often taken second place to my "doing."

In a nation where our economy gives worth to the individual, we all sense the lure of being busy. So many of us feel almost embarrassed to say that we are free any particular evening. Many others feel equally embarrassed to answer questions about what they've been up to with answers such as, "Just reading a book."

In recognizing this, it is important that we seek a balance between "doing" and "being," making sure that a vibrant relationship with God motivates each of our compassionate acts. We must be certain that we are not just doing, doing, and doing that we might find a sense of worth.

In a most insightful statement on this subject, Henri Nouwen wrote in *A Reflection on the Christian Life*:

> In our society, which equates worth with productivity, patient action is very difficult. We seem so concerned with doing something worthwhile, bringing about changes, planning, organizing, structuring and manufacturing that we often forget that it is not we who redeems but God. To be busy, "where the action is" and "on top of things" often seem to have become goals in themselves. We then have forgotten our vocation is not to give visibility to our powers but to God's compassion.

How and why we make and deliver the cake lies deep within us. God has either redeemed and restored us, or he has not. He has either converted and sanctified our past, with all its needy, grabby, possessive insistence, or he has not.

So many times while I have been in conversation with someone, the Holy Spirit has cautioned and prevented me, whispering into the "ear" of my heart, "Dan, don't say that. It will not honor me." Each time I hear and obey (or for that matter, bake and deliver the cake with right motive and without expectation of accolades), I demonstrate the purity of my being, which God has sanctified with his presence.

The one gifted with compassion is responsible to understand the motive for his or her actions and to guard carefully the purity of the motive. That person will pray something like this: "Lord, in this act may I be the deliverer of your presence. May they see you and you only. May they understand your love and care for them."

It is possible that our need to be needed, fueled and glorified by busyness, can become an end in itself—until, that is, we are struck and stopped by the Spirit's quiet voice within, asking, "Is this for you, or is this for me?"

Can I take that cake to my neighbor wanting visibility for myself? The answer is, "Certainly!" But praise God, I can also do it as an expression of his love carried out by his messenger, who will receive his reward.

The *Real* Bread of Life

None of us would dispute the truth of the words of Jesus when he proclaimed himself to be the "bread of life" (John 6:35). But sometimes we are tempted to elevate ourselves to be the "bread of life" for those in need.

How different that is from the one of humble spirit who arrives—whether cloaked as a police chaplain, a nurse, a neighbor, or a friend—bearing the very presence of Christ, seeking only that God might be glorified.

The world is too filled with "I." *I* will be there. *I* will rescue. *I* will be the helper. *I* will be their bread of life. But Jesus' words become cautionary for us: "*I* am the bread of life." In other words, there is only one Bread of Life, and we're not him!

At one critical time in my years of ministry, the Holy Spirit spoke and said to me, "If you seek to be the bread of life for them, you will be consumed." Again, cautionary words, followed by this warning: "You cannot do this without me. I have appointed you, and I will empower you. I will not share my glory with you, nor will I allow you to continue if you seek to take it for yourself. Put away your ID, your 'officialness,' and be my humble servant. Give me to them. They need me. Love them with and through my Spirit."

I found those words liberating. I realized I don't *have* to serve God with my gift of compassion; I *get* to serve him. I knew that I didn't have to be adequate, whatever that meant, because he already is. I was liberated and set free to act as the local "breadman," delivering the true "Bread of Life."

I was free...free to give of the gift of compassion God has given me. And those with whom I came in contact through my ministry were just as free to receive.

CHAPTER 6

The Cost of Compassion...
Today

Chaplaincy was the context in which I exercised the God-given gift of compassion. For me, it was the perfect place. Each day as I drove to ministry (I never called it *work*), I thought about what a privilege it was to serve that way. But I also realized that along with the incredible privilege came a lot of pain. That is why I came to call chaplaincy a "painful privilege."

While the wonder and privilege of being involved in delivering gifts of compassionate service are so often very real and plain to see, the costs of practicing compassion are very real as well. In my arena of practice they often seemed *too* real, *too* stark, and *too* painful. These words of Henri Nouwen in *The Wounded Healer* rang true for me in my ministry:

> It seems necessary to re-establish the basic principle that no one can help anyone without becoming involved, without entering with his whole person into the painful situation, without taking the risk of becoming hurt, wounded, or even destroyed in the process.

Some of the costs of practicing compassion are very immediate—they are paid *today*. For those who are yet young in life or perhaps young in the exercise of the gift of compassion, the first cost extracted is often a loss of innocence.

The Loss of Innocence

Most of us enter the world wanted, even if we were not expected. As infants, we grow with the firm knowledge that love surrounds us, cares for us, and protects us. A cry brings food, loving touch, or the removal of a wet diaper. As children, love brings a wiped nose, an encouraging word, and a loving hug. And our parents tenderly love and care for us into our teenage years, when we begin stretching boundaries in preparation for independence.

As children, most of us are innocent of the knowledge of inequity, pain, suffering, and evil. For some of us, the loss of innocence may come in the subtle realization that there are people whose lives are jolted and jarred, moment to moment, day in and day out, by the evil that surrounds them. For others, however, this loss of innocence is anything but subtle. It comes as the result of a violent act that cuts, bruises, and bleeds the inner psyche—to be remembered forever.

Those with the gift of compassion first recognize the reality of evil, unfairness, pain, or wounds suffered by their fellow travelers. Then they are continually reminded of what is bad about this world. The firefighter or police officer runs toward danger while all others run away. Likewise, the compassionate one is drawn, as if by a magnet, toward the pain of others. Each contact brings another assault on innocence.

The Good Samaritan (Luke 10:25-37) was drawn to a man who lay wounded and bleeding beside the road. The inner gift of this compassionate one pulled him to respond and help, and not to pass by on the other side of the road, as so many others had done. Something within him moved him toward helping when no one else would.

Every one of our Good Samaritan responses—the kind of responses Jesus exemplified with this story—reminds us that evil, inequity, pain, suffering, and "piling on" happen to people. We cannot escape that reality. The compassionate responder can sometimes feel that life is filled with nothing but pain, that nothing is fair, that suffering is everywhere, and that everything and everyone is evil—or if not evil, then at least suspect of being evil.

In July 1996 I wrote

Dear Friends across America:

Church was a welcome respite from the week. The morning message was appropriate, as it dealt with evil in the world. But the words of the song leader were unforgettable as we prepared to sing, "I'm standing on holy ground...." He reminded us that he was not talking about the church sanctuary but everywhere we had been. "Think of all of the places you have been this past week," he said. And I did.

We sat in the detective's car the night the little girl's body was found, and I prayed. "Lord, make this place where evil has happened into a sacred place as these people come and work here for the next several hours." *Holy Ground*...even that place of evil...where God is present with/in his people.

Oh yes, there is evil. Sometimes it is so blatant, so "in your face," that I want to run from it and never again be confronted by it. But that is not to be. Stand there, take it, question it, and cry over it. But it is not ours to run from. It is ours to wade into and stand against. It is ours to overcome with good—and we do. How else do you deal with the brutal murder of an innocent child? How else do you sleep at night? How else do you function effectively when that is demanded?

Justice will prevail, but it will not bring little Cynthia back. She will be entrusted to the tender care of the God who said, "Allow the little children to come to me...for such is the kingdom of God." Pray for Cynthia's family and friends. Also, please remember our chaplain who is ministering to them.

❖

It costs the compassionate one dearly every time he or she journeys to stare into the face of evil, pain, and suffering. We are reminded again that innocence is now for us a fairy tale, so long gone that it seems as if it never was. Whether by the bedside of an emaciated, dying person, or on the killing ground of a homicide scene, the compassionate one stands again with outstretched hands, accepting the call to share in the pain.

The Shedding of Blood

Blood is life-giving and life-preserving, and in the right circumstances it is beautiful. It is beautiful as it courses unseen through our bodies and provides the sustenance of life. But blood that pours forth from wounds is not beautiful. It is ugly and scary.

By the time I arrived at most crime scenes, the blood was most often coagulated in streaks across the victim or pooled beneath that dreadfully wounded head. The ugliness of the blood was a brutal reminder that there had once been life but now it was gone. *They are not home*, or *It is now only the shell*, I often thought to myself, and somehow that made it easier.

But the blood, now only a part of what remained to be cleaned up, was there. While ugly and awful, gross and disgusting, it had to be dealt with. In the early days, often the chaplains, feeling compassion upon the families, would clean up the mess of blood from the home. It was the least we could do. But at what price? What would we see and what would we feel as towels, water, soap, sprays, disinfectants, and carpet cleaners turned the dark crimson to a frothy pink to be thrown away down a drain or into plastic bags for disposal?

On February 13, 1987, I wrote

Dear Friends across America:

May I depart from the normal format of a story or two and share with you words that speak so deeply inside of me? They purify me, they motivate me, and they test what I am made of. These words are truth, truth explained, truth that finds its demonstration all around me every day....

"It is the nature of love to insinuate itself into the sorrow and sins of others. It is bound to mourn. It has the doom of bleeding on it. And rightly so, for 'When we cease to bleed we cease to bless.'" (E. Stanley Jones, *The Christ of the Mount*)

Hear it again, "When we cease to bleed we cease to bless." Bleed with the man who was a shotgun suicide...bleed with his family and those who must come and investigate and clean up that which remains. Bleed with the parents of the son who dies in a filthy apartment of a heroin overdose. Bleed with the parents of the nine-month-old who dies of SIDS. Love bleeds with those who bleed. Love rejoices with those who rejoice. Love lays down its life for its friends.

◇

It may be the blood of the one in need of compassion, or it may be the blood of the compassionate one. In the garden, Jesus sweat "like drops of blood falling to the ground" (Luke 22:44) in his grief and agony over the world and the impending Cross. The delivery of compassion can be a similar exercise for us. To "suffer with" another who physically bleeds that life-threatening flow means to bleed within ourselves—as if our lives were also at stake. To watch their life ebb away is to feel a bit of our own slip away as well. While they may go away into eternity, we return to our home with another wound, with another emotional "bleed"...until our healing comes.

The danger for those of us who exercise the gift of compassion is spiritual and emotional anemia, which happens as we bleed and bleed and do not get regularly transfused. Or we bleed so frequently that no amount of transfusing can keep up with the loss.

The Shedding of Tears

The cost of ministering compassion will very often be tears. A fellow chaplain and friend of mine, Landis Epp, says, "Tears are the price we pay for the privilege of loving." Tears—I love them...I hate them. Somewhere in God's creative plan, he connected our hearts with our tear ducts. Tears have a purpose far beyond just moistening our eyes so our eyelids don't stick to our eyeballs; they have an emotional connection. While I don't fully understand that connection, I frequently experience it for myself.

On July 15, 2002, I wrote

We stood in a circle, the other chaplains and I. I prayed, and the tears came. I cried. I cried for our common calling—law enforcement chaplaincy. I cried for our collective experiences. I cried for the loss of the deputy from their department. I had just written a newsletter article about tears, and there I went again, shedding some more.

Sometimes I am self-conscious of my tears, but I am never ashamed of them. They were not a part of my genetic makeup and they were not learned behavior from my family of origin, but they were still a very real part of my life. They are there, for everyone to see, even as I stand in front of a banner that loudly proclaims, "Real Men Don't Cry." And I say, "Oh yes they do!"

I was with a "real man" a few weeks ago at lunch. He is one of the world's fine human beings, and we enjoy lunch together from time to time. Oddly enough, one of the topics of conversation that day was tears. It is one thing among many that we share.

I think that is one of the reasons we are friends. I recognized that in him when we met some twenty years ago—that his tears were as close to the surface as mine. During our many years of friendship, we had never talked about our propensity to tears, but that day, over some good teriyaki, we talked tears. No, I don't mean the breakout bawling, fall-on-the-floor, sobbing kind of tears. We talked about the kind that flow from your heart, slip from the corner of your eyes, and slide down your cheeks ever so quietly.

Those tears come so readily. A quiet moment watching television and a Hallmark ad comes on, tears slide down. I am unsuspectingly driving down the street and I get ambushed by a man in the crosswalk. He is gently holding his little daughter (I guessed that) in her pink snowsuit. She looked my way and waved her fat little dimpled hand at me. The tears slide down again. Happy tears like that are really kind of fun and sure do feel good.

There are the tears that come from the awful circumstances of life, the kind of circumstances to which the police, firefighters, and chaplains respond. They are never happy things. The fire burns down the "Hallmark home," and the little girl is shamefully abused and beaten by her father. The tears that come in those moments are tears hot with anger, frustration, and bewilderment, tears that ask, "How could he?"

But why do I tear up so often and so readily? The explanation seems so simple. When the barrel is full, it only takes one more drop to make it overflow. The explanation to my friend was that simple and that quick. That is why we shed tears in happy times as well as sad. Our barrels are full. His is full from his orphan childhood, two tours in Vietnam, a failed marriage, and lots of years in law enforcement. Mine is full from childhood experiences, blessings that are mine without reason (mine without deserving them), and thirty years of tending to broken hearts and broken bodies as a police chaplain.

I have often felt like I am full of tears to that line that is marked on the barrel just below where my eyes are. Is that abnormal? Am I neurotic, certifiably mentally ill, suffering from posttraumatic stress disorder, secondary traumatization, delayed posttraumatic stress, or one of those other conditions given a fancy name that has taken on new meaning in recent years? No, I don't think so. I will admit to some compassion fatigue settling in at this thirty-year mark, but not the other stuff.

As I stood in the circle of those chaplains the other day, ringing in my ears were their almost offhand comments about the calls they recently had. I know chaplaincy calls, and all of them have to do with dead people—people dead by homicide, suicide, accident, hanging, shooting, stabbing, burning, or beating. And that isn't even the worst of it. The worst of it, worse than what happened to the dead person, is dealing with the grieving family members left behind. It is dealing with their tears of anguish, disappointment, hurt, hopelessness, helplessness, and profound sudden loss, all of which leave them to be swept up into a basket and held there until the crisis passes and they can begin to function again.

That is what fills the barrel—dealing so frequently with those left behind that there is no time to grieve in between torturous encounters. There is not time to drain the barrel, and so it continues to fill until every day, every moment of every day, one more drop and the barrel overflows.

Are tears a bad thing? No, the tears are the draining of the barrel, at the appropriate time and in the appropriate place. The level of the barrel goes down and is ready and able to take in some more.

My friend—you who share teriyaki or Mongolian beef or whatever we have for lunch—let's continue to be sensitive to our world, sensitive enough to shed tears. My fellow chaplains, please do the same. Please keep emptying those barrels so you can continue to do those most important things you do. Let us remember, when we shed tears we are in good company: "Jesus wept" (John 11:35).

◇

The apostle Paul said it so well: "Rejoice with those who rejoice, and weep with those who weep" (Romans 12:15 NASB). There is no better way to identify with another, to enter into his or her pain, to show empathy, and to "suffer with" than to "weep with those who weep."

I have never been guilty of "falling apart" at the scene of any tragedy or crisis, only guilty (if that is what it could be called) of being human enough to feel that mother's or father's pain so deeply that my heart connected with my eyes, showing that I cared.

Those tears are the price I pay for my God-given gift of compassion, and it's a price I pay easily and willingly.

Grief

Grief: "Keen mental suffering or distress over affliction or loss...." That sounds like a simple definition, all right. But grief is an emotion that fills more than a sentence, more than a page, even more than a book. It may fill a lifetime, and for some it does. Over the years of my working life, I have suffered grief—grief *of* others, grief *with* others—and it became my own. Grief, like fine sand in a dust storm, can invade every opening of your life and cover your entire being with its gritty pollution. Left in place, the grit of grief can wear down the moving parts of life until life itself will not function.

*On April 10, 1986, I wrote for my
newsletter and titled it* Little Babies

Dear Friends across America:

I watched the little baby a lot during the evening church service that we were in...chubby, coal-black hair with a little barrette that just matched in color her tiny outfit of deep lavender. Judi and I both wanted to grab her and run. Later we sat with her family and enjoyed "pie and conversation"...conversation that often turned to kids and turned our eyes back on the now-sleeping little doll that had captured our hearts. You know, it's hard to forget a little baby like that...like that one I saw just this morning. Skin the color of ivory, pale as milk. Bright blue

eyes that stood out as big as marbles—deeply recessed, they
were the prominent feature of this six-month-old baby girl's
face. A light, soft coating of the finest of hair covered her head
but did not cover the bruises...bruises being examined by the
pathologist as he sought the cause of death of this little one.

I stood transfixed as I watched those hands so gently turn the
quiet little figure dwarfed by the large stainless steel table she
lay on. My heart cried out, "Would to God that she were cuddled
down in a warm bassinet with the hands of her mommy turning
her to more comfortable sleep." But sleep it was not. The detective and I talked quietly until my heart was too pained to stay
longer. My business there was done and I walked out into the
brilliant spring sunshine with dark clouds brewing in my heart.

That now-familiar pain rose in the depths of my stomach. I felt
it come and then pass as I drove on toward the precinct. I've
wondered why cops become hard and businesslike about their
job, but today I know...it hurts a whole bunch when you are not.
It hurts when you are "on the surface" with your emotions and
willingly accept the pain in your heart and mind...it hurts a lot.

I see the hands of Jesus reaching out as he says, "Whoever
welcomes one of these little children in my name welcomes
me." But Jesus, what of one who does not welcome one of these
little ones? What of one who neglects, abuses, and brings to
death one of these tiny little bundles?

There is nothing left for this day but a prayer for this tiny "blue
eyes": "Lord Jesus, receive the spirit of this child, give her the
love and care, gentle caresses, and soft spoken words she did
not receive on this earth. Restore in the resurrection this tiny
body to perfection and bring sights of wondrous joy to her bluest
of eyes."

◇

In chaplaincy, grief seems to be the order of the day...for
nearly every day. They don't call the chaplain when the son
gets straight A's at school. They call when the son has just mur-
dered his sister or has himself been killed in a late-night auto
accident. Grief, thick with pain, fear, and anxiety, pervades the

life experience until it is resolved by forgiveness, talked out, dulled by time, or medicated into oblivion.

The compassionate one—the one who "suffers with"— suffers the depth of grief, albeit not as the parents suffer, but only in that part they shared. Over and over, the compassionate one shares the grief with innumerable victims until, saturated with it, he or she becomes, as Jesus, "a man of sorrows and acquainted with grief."

CHAPTER 7

The Cost of Compassion... Tomorrow

Pain gripped my stomach; I felt the beginnings of "Montezuma's Revenge"...and we weren't even in Mexico yet.

It was December 12, 1985. I knew where the physical pain came from: the aftermath of the emotional and spiritual pain that had surrounded and completely permeated my last two weeks. The "Spanaway Jr. High Incident" was now two weeks history and my wife, Judi, and I were winging off to a long-before-arranged trip to Mexico. I had been a volunteer chaplain with police and fire for fifteen years, about a year-and-a-half full time, but this was the first time I recognized that this work could take a real toll on me personally.

Without fanfare or "bolts of lightning" God spoke through the pain of my stomach and the drone of the jet engines: "This kind of ministry could shorten your life. Are you willing to pay that price?" Without thought, I answered him within myself, "Yes, I am." And I meant it.

That day, and each of the grief- and tragedy-filled days to come, I realized that I would not only pay costs each day, but also face long-term, "tomorrow" costs.

The long-term costs of exercising compassion often have very academic names such as vicarious victimization, delayed stress reaction, or posttraumatic stress disorder. While they may be referred to in such intellectual, softened terms of psychological jargon, they are, in reality, much more stark, mundane, and hard.

Delayed Stress Reaction

What a great day it was. After a very stressful week, it was now Saturday, my day to do the too-long-neglected home tasks. The project for this day was finishing up the fence. All I needed to do was put the hardware on the gate. I jumped in the van, drove to the local hardware store, and easily found and purchased the hinges, screws, and latch I needed.

As I drove home along 356th, a line of cars was slowing down. But I was doing my usual Saturday zone-out and nothing mattered to me as I relaxed and enjoyed the ease of the day. Before long I came upon the reason for the slowdown: A young lady was kneeling down beside an injured dog.

It's a Dalmatian, I observed to myself. Our family had owned one, and we had come to call them "damnations." I never particularly liked that breed of dog because they seem high-strung. But from what I could see, this particular dog didn't appear to be too badly hurt and would likely be on its way home soon.

About a block past this scene, it hit me; I began to cry. It was not a tear-sliding-down-the-cheek kind of cry; it was racking sobs that shook my body so hard I could scarcely stay on the road. My mind questioned, *What is happening to me? I don't even like Dalmatians! Nolta, get control of yourself!* Finally, I got hold of myself and went on home, feeling freakish and bewildered at my sudden outburst of tears.

As I walked into the house I started to tell Judi what had just happened to me...only to have the sobs begin again. Seldom has my wife seen me in that state. She held me as I tried to explain what I had just experienced. Totally without understanding, I feared I was having some kind of a nervous breakdown.

Not until the tears ended and I had gone back to my fence project—still feeling a little confused—did it dawn on me what was going on. It had been a very stressful week; it wasn't the injured dog that had me such a wreck.

On the Friday night before, I had written

I was hard at work at my desk in the Lakewood Precinct when the call came from Dispatch. "Sergeant Adams is requesting you respond and notify the family of a young man who has set fire to himself in his car. He has been airlifted to Harborview in Seattle, and we need to get his family on the way." Cold names, addresses, and facts do not even begin to tell the story of what I knew I would find at the end of that "dark alley" of a call.

As I drove, my mind began to fashion the picture of horror...*Set himself on fire in his car?* Airlifted to Harborview Hospital could only mean he is in very tough shape—his life is threatened.

Who will be at the house? I wondered. I soon found out. I was met at the door by a very dignified, well-dressed, middle-aged black woman...the young man's mother. At that moment, she was his closest relative at home. His wife and two little girls were away. With the news came the despair of what her son had done, despair for his life, and despair for his little family. The story tumbled out as she hastily prepared for the trip to Seattle. He had been a Marine, assigned to the guarding of a United States Embassy in one of the African countries. He had met and married his wife and now they had two little girls...and lots of problems.

The mother, a school principal, competent and proud, refused my offer of transportation to Seattle and left for the hospital. The incident would not end with the notification, and I soon learned from Sergeant Adams the story as it was pieced together. A can of lawnmower gas, removed from his parents' garage, a short trip to a vacant lot nearby...he poured the gas over himself and struck a match. The gas ignited and he was quickly engulfed in the searing flames. The pain and panic drove him from the car, and the opening of the door poured fresh oxygen into its interior. The remaining gasoline exploded, burning him horribly. The responding firefighters quickly recognized his peril and called for Medivac. It was already too late for this young man. His life was about to end.

I saw none of it. I did not go to the vacant lot or see him or the car. But later that day I saw *them*. I saw the dark beauty of the young wife. I saw two of the most beautiful little girls I have ever seen. I heard their anguish, fear, and despair. I saw their tears and cried with them.

Rooted in family problems, his death would forever lay at the feet of his young wife. That day the first of the tears, which would continue for months, if not years, began to flow. Presence, prayers, and some very special Teddy bears for the girls were the best I could do that day.

...and the next day was Saturday.

⬧

Just as sin does not collect its wage immediately when we "fall," "critical incident stress" does not manifest itself in the life of the compassionate one immediately after he or she is in a place of assisting the suffering. Sometimes it breaks out a few days later (as in my case), and sometimes it takes weeks, months, or even years to wear you down, weave its way through your guts, and then burst out into the open. When that happens, all of the emotions, which before had been kept under guard, may break out of their prison and show themselves as if the incident had just happened. Fear, tremors, gasping for breath, and the tears come forth, leaving the once well-guarded quivering with the question, "What is this all about?"

My emotional reaction upon seeing the injured Dalmatian was all about moving through too many crises too quickly and never giving my mind and heart enough time to "catch up" and process the emotions as they built up within me. The dog was the "last straw," and all I had held in from previous incidents, including Friday's immolation, came bursting forth.

Posttraumatic Stress Disorder

His name is Ben. I helped train him many years ago, but today two chaplains sit in yet another training session. This one is a hot topic: posttraumatic stress disorder (PTSD). During the class, Ben quietly leaned over to me and said, "That's me." I understood what he meant; he fit all the descriptors of PTSD. I knew Ben as a very competent, concerned, and caring chaplain, but I did not know of his quiet struggle over the past several months.

This is Ben's story, in his own words

In January of 1988 God called me to be an emergency service chaplain serving in Whitman County, Washington. The only knowledge I had of posttraumatic stress disorder was that it was something the Vietnam vets claimed to have.

I soon discovered that posttraumatic stress is something that chaplains and emergency responders face each day that they go to work. Even though I saw awful sights and helped people through the worst part of their lives, I was sustained by the knowledge that God had called me to this ministry. It was a delight to be able to serve him in this way. I loved my job and got excited when I was dispatched to go on a call.

The longer I served as a chaplain in that rural county and made many friends, the more difficult it became because I responded to the deaths of friends or their family members. As the years went by I could put names on the crosses that popped up along both the highways and county roads. I could tell you which houses had domestic violence or where someone had committed suicide.

While I worked as a full-time chaplain, I served as a firefighter for Colfax Fire to supplement my income. A part of my duty was to assist with our high school cadet program. I knew all the cadets fairly well. On a rainy spring day in April of 1996 I was called to a head-on collision between a semi truck and a car. The car was mangled, and we were not able to see the driver well enough to identify her. We came to the conclusion that the car belonged to one of our cadets. The state trooper in charge of the scene believed that if I crawled under the car and looked up I might be able to verify her identity. I did crawl under the car and determined that it was the sixteen-year-old cadet. I went to her home and notified her parents.

Following that car accident, something in me began to die. My enthusiasm for being a chaplain was not as great as it had been. During the next year I continued to function as a chaplain. I began to back away from the fire department and was no longer involved with the cadets. By April of 1997, I was only responding to calls as a chaplain, not as a firefighter.

On Good Friday in April of 1997, I responded to a truck fire in which the driver had been burned to death. Arriving on scene, I saw a close friend who told me the driver was his best friend. I did not know the driver well, but I could put a name to a face in my memory bank. After everyone had left I assisted the coroner and a deputy in removing the torso.

One month later, I was called to a spray-plane crash with fire. The pilot was not hurt in the crash itself but died as a result of the fire that followed. An acquaintance of mine had seen the crash and attempted to remove the pilot from the plane. I debriefed the witnesses and firefighters.

That night, I crossed over a line. Something in me started to rebel to my responding as a chaplain. Death notifications became a chore. When I heard of accidents on the highway, I would go the opposite direction. I would find excuses for not going to work. I lost my sense of humor. I am a "people person," but I no longer wanted to be with anyone. The relationship between my wife and me suffered as I isolated myself even from her. I had enjoyed speaking in churches and telling them about my job as a chaplain. It was no longer easy to do that, so I quit speaking in churches. I talked to my doctor, who was also my friend. He put me on Prozac and suggested I take some time off. I did, but my life continued to go downhill.

In July of that year, I attended the annual training seminar of the International Conference of Police Chaplains. I took a class on police burnout. I soon realized that I had all of the symptoms that the instructor had said were evident in police officers....

❖

Ben's story does not end there. He visited a counselor in a nearby city, but his explanation of what he had been through was met with, "Don't tell me that kind of stuff. I can't listen to it." Ben was in trouble when he came to the training seminar. A long talk between us followed the class. I was able to put Ben in contact with a psychologist in our area who worked with us on our Critical Incident Stress Management Team. Ben was diagnosed with full-blown PTSD. He drove 250 miles to our area each week for a number of weeks, and Dr. Ratcliffe was able to help him. After three years, he was restored to chaplaincy service.

Vietnam veterans (or any combat vet), police officers, firefighters, emergency room personnel, chaplains—anyone who experiences trauma and crisis up close and personal—are vulnerable to PTSD. The symptoms are more severe than compassion fatigue and more deeply imbedded; the difference is akin to a car wearing out versus having it blow an engine. I don't know all the finer clinical details of PTSD, but I know enough to understand that it is severe and debilitating, and that it can become life-threatening—emotionally if not physically.

Compassion Fatigue

"I have bled out, and it is time to go." Those were not the words I *said* at my retirement, but they describe how I *felt* at that time. Over the years, I had heard descriptive terms like "wearing out for God" but never "bleeding out for God." But now I understood how that felt. I had bled out.

In my studies of stress—both academic and by personal experience—I had heard of compassion fatigue. But a time finally came when I had to admit I had it. I cannot even tell you when I first became aware of its symptoms, which include a constant preoccupation with crisis events, avoidance, numbing, and weariness. At first, I passed the weariness off as just simple fatigue, telling myself, "There have been too many calls lately." Writing has always been my therapy, and now I can look back and see the heaviness begin to set in.

On January 27, 1999, I wrote

Dear Friends across America:

From time to time I am particularly touched in my spirit by another human being—"another human being" meaning one born to my species; another person, another creation of God who is loved by him but forgotten by most of his or her fellow humans.

I met her at 0330 the other morning. She had her own furnished apartment. She had a television set, a stereo, and even a remote control. There was no evidence that she was without food. Yet she touched my heart and soul.

I didn't ask her age—not polite, you know—but I would guess she was about fifty. She looked sixty-five. Her apartment was jammed full of "stuff," with just enough room to walk around what passed for a coffee table. I steered her toward a chair, moved some things off the couch, and seated myself. The deputy stood near the door.

After confirming that she knew the man, I proceeded in as gently but as firm a way as I could to tell her that her friend was dead (a suicide about two hours before). Confusion and questions followed my sad announcement. The tears came tumbling over the questions, and I began to get the picture.

This lady was now ALONE. I had just told her that one of the only friends she had in the world had just committed suicide by jumping from a nearby freeway overpass into the path of an oncoming semi. She would never see him again. He would never drink coffee with her again. She would never, ever, ever, hear his voice calling from the adjoining apartment. She was alone.

A few minutes and a shared prayer later, I stepped out into the cold early-morning hours, frankly glad to be out of the smoke-filled apartment. Now she was out of my sight. But she was not out of my mind...or my heart.

The district chaplain who followed up with her yesterday was not invited inside. She told him she was leaving to move to Texas. Please follow her with your prayers.

❖

I later titled this newsletter *Alone*. As I reflect on it, I remember well being out on that very cold night in that very bad neighborhood and realizing, maybe for the first time, that I really did not want to be there, knowing the pain I would likely face. Was it the weariness from so many other calls over so many years, or was it just *this* call? Was it the hour of the night, or had there just been too many nights? Was it this lady's being alone that bothered me, or was it my own sense of loneliness?

I have long known that for me a sense of loneliness accompanies grief. Perhaps it is the uniqueness of what I do. Perhaps it is the taking on of another's sense of loneliness in their grief. The pervading sense of loneliness was a part of my compassion fatigue, and the fact that this woman was now so very much alone magnified my own loneliness and began deepening my fatigue. Whatever else it is, compassion fatigue is loneliness.

Henri Nouwen made a profound observation about the loneliness he bears: "The awareness of loneliness reveals to us an inner emptiness that can be destructive when misunderstood, but filled with promise for him who can tolerate its sweet pain" (*The Wounded Healer*).

While the loneliness was a terrible pain that no proximity of others could overcome, that very pain drove me—and drives others gifted with compassion—into the "field" again and again to meet with the freshly wounded one who feels so alone. The joining of two lonely ones provides a fresh touch of healing for both. Two kindred spirits connect, one having come to help and the other so desperately needing a helper. In that vacuum of need, a bond forms, a "friend" is found, and both have a need met.

One of my assignments at the sheriff's department included teaching stress management to the new-hire deputies and corrections officers. I talked to them about how they as new-hires would be so eager to respond to every call—*over*eager to respond. I would tell them that during the first few years on the job they would feel that they just couldn't wait for the next call, for the next time they got to flip on the lights and siren and "four-bell" off to the emergency. I would describe times when that same kind of call would end up being just another bank robbery. And then, I said, a time would come when the call that had once excited them would be a major annoyance in their day.

The same thing so often happens to the compassionate helper. The horrible, repeated often enough, falls flat. The stimulation threshold is moved up another notch; it takes more to get the adrenaline flowing. The giver willingly dives in deeper, and the awful becomes the routine.

How is it possible that such terrible circumstances can become routine? In the "normal" world it would not, but it can in the world of the emergency responder or the chaplain. But can it be so routine that you begin to do it automatically; or do it without the needed and necessary compassion? Yes, it can, and unfortunately it often does.

Here is what I am talking about:

Compassion fatigue is functioning on "empty." While extreme giving can often push the giver to the point of feeling "empty," there are also cases where the demands and needs of the hurting can "overfill" even the most compassionate giver. In a case like that, that person reasons, "I don't have to think. I have done it so many times." When that happens, the giver may well "do" the things needed but will often fail to "be" what is needed—a compassionate, feeling helper.

Compassion fatigue is functioning numb. When the work of rescuing and helping becomes routine for the compassionate one, he or she may begin to function in a state of numbness. When the wounds of the injured one are struck over and over, the nerves that have been pummeled into submission can cease to function, leaving that person numb and unable to feel. For the compassionate one, actually entering into the pain of others over and over can have a similar numbing effect, which can be the death knell of effective responding. The very gift of compassion lies at the core of effective helping, and when the helper can no longer summon the compassion, he or she is no better than the one who responds without compassion, one whose "helping" is more "clinical" or "professional" then truly "human."

Compassion fatigue is avoidance. An unrecognizable, unmarked time can come when the pain of practicing compassion becomes greater than the privilege. In my case, I arrived at a time when I began to look harder for another chaplain to take the call. I did not want to admit I didn't want to go; before, I had always eagerly awaited the next call. Partly in recognition, partly as a defense mechanism, and partly as a natural progression of my career, I began to do more administrative work, began training more chaplains, and became even more immersed in the International Conference of Police Chaplains and the international chaplaincy. All good and useful work, it prolonged my "life expectancy" as a chaplain, but I did some of it as a result of compassion fatigue.

I have been told that compassion fatigue is not a treatable illness and that the only thing I could do to relieve it was to take a break and get away for an extended period of time. But is it preventable? Here I fight my own head. If compassion is the gift that draws me to those suffering, and if compassion means "to suffer with"—and it most certainly means that—then how do we stop the effects of compassion fatigue, especially when we continue to take on the suffering of others?

Perhaps among these suggestions lies a solution. I should have gathered more people around me to share my suffering. I should have had more diverse activities in my life. I should have been less "vulnerable" to the pain of others. I should have seen a professional counselor or sought out a close confidant with whom I could share regularly. I should have prayed more.

I should have...but I didn't.

Even today I ask myself, "If I had refused to 'suffer with' and instead just gone and been physically present but emotionally aloof, could I have done it longer?" Ultimately, my answer is this: Maybe I would have lasted longer, but I would not and could not have been satisfied with the results. It would not have worked for the victims and their families, and it would not have satisfied the inner cry of my own heart to truly meet the needs before me. I would never have been satisfied with the work God had given me if I had tried to do it without the measure of compassion, if I hadn't suffered with those to whom I was called.

The extremes of being compassionate and enduring the pain of another versus being objective and keeping distance from the victim make it seem as though there is never a "comfortable" meeting place.

There is, however, an answer, and that answer is to maintain the inner joy of the Lord, despite the circumstances of life.

In December 1986, I wrote Joy of the Lord

"What do you want for Christmas, Dan...Dad...Mr. Nolta?" (Depending on who is doing the asking) What *do* I want? That is hard for me to say. Clothes are nice, but I already have more than I wear. A gadget would be fun, but when would I use it? So my mind goes as I try to make a list for wife and kids and anybody else who cares.

The real truth is, all my material needs are taken care of and my wants are either too foolish to mention or impossible to think about.

Before you write me off as self-satisfied and conceited, let me be very candid about needs beyond the material. There is a Christmas song that begins, "Joy to the world, the Lord is come...." That speaks to my innermost need, which a new tie or some shaving lotion can never meet.

This last week, it was dealing with the family of a fifteen-year-old suicide victim. The week before, it was the aftermath of a double homicide that claimed my attention. Heart-stopping, gut-wrenching grief was overwhelming. There was not even a glimmer of a smile to be seen in those faces, just tears and bewildered pain.

I am well aware that happiness is in short supply for the victims and their families we work with. I can handle that only if my own level of inner joy can be maintained. That was resupplied last week following the suicide (more about that next month). It said to me again, "Dan, if you are going to do this, you must maintain your inner joy."

Go to the shelf and look at the joy supply! Getting low on joy? Spend some time with your wife, count your blessings, think about your kids, remember who put you here. And if that is not enough, I know the real "Joy Wholesaler."

Nehemiah tells me, "The joy of the Lord is your strength."
Psalms tells me, "In his presence is fullness of joy." And the
book of Job demonstrates, "...and sorrow is turned into joy."

My Christmas list will read: gray slacks, new ties, air compres-
sor, NIV study Bible, Mercedes 450 SL. But even in having all of
those, my real need will continue to be constant inner joy to
help me stand in this place, doing exactly what the Christ of
Christmas wants me to do.

❖

Maintaining that inner joy was most difficult for me. Early
on, Judi said to me, "You don't laugh as much as you used to."
It was true. I found myself identifying with the Old Testament
description of Jesus: "A man of sorrows and acquainted with
grief."

The time came when the only thing I could do was to get
away from it. And I have. No more midnight trips to do death
notifications. No more fatality accidents. No more dead babies.
I still love chaplains and the chaplaincy and all they do, so I've
given my energies over to training other chaplains and writing
so that they may remain healthy, so that they might have long
and productive careers as law enforcement or fire chaplains.

While compassion fatigue helped to end my career as an
active "middle-of-the-night" chaplain, it has not ended my caring. It's just moved it to another arena.

CHAPTER 8

The Rewards of Compassion

How many times have I been caused to reflect on the words of E. Stanley Jones? Most often it was in the dark of night, usually after a very late call out and an even later drive home as I thought about what I had just done and the victims and victim families I had been with. Mingled with those feelings of sadness and grief was a sense of satisfaction and gratitude that I'd had the opportunity to be with them. In spite of the pain-filled evening I always knew that "when the bell rang" I would be ready to go again.

One passage from E. Stanley Jones has a special place in my life and in my ministry:

> Now those that mourn are comforted. The strange thing happens that those who deliberately take on themselves trouble and pain in behalf of others find happiness—they are comforted. The most absolutely happy people of the world are those who choose to care till it hurts.
>
> —*The Christ of the Mount*

To even speak of compassion in terms of personal gain or reward seems to cheapen its expression. At the same time, God's promises carry us through the appointed ministry to the results, one of which is that he rewards and blesses those who are compassionate.

Now, after so many years in my ministry, it is easier for me to think of the blessings or rewards of living a life of compassion. I can honestly say that on some days, when the demands placed on me were front and center and time was short or a situation hard, it would have been easier to have had the gift of administration. But as I look back on the years gone by and reflect on all I have experienced, I am so thankful that God allowed and enabled me to be where I was for so many years. The privilege of being on the front lines—in combat—and allowing God's gift of compassion to flow through me found its own reward.

In July 1992 I wrote in my newsletter

Eight years down and heading into year number nine, are my thoughts today as I write. These last eight years have gone so quickly, as my life has been enriched by the relationships and experiences.

How could my life not have been enriched? How could it not be, when I am where God wants me to be? How could it not be when I am at the Pierce County Sheriff's Department?

I have found that I love this department and the people in it. My relationship with some of them is yet stiff and formal, but with most of them it is friend, brother, or, with the younger ones, father.

And the experiences I have had....How can you measure what it means to be with people in their hour of pain so deep that they feel as if their hearts have been ripped from them?

How can I describe my evolving feelings of what it means to stand beside a now-lifeless body? That person—that human being, father, husband, lover—was a few minutes or hours before so very much alive and unsuspecting of what was to be.

How can I help but have a growing sense of the sacredness of life or, for that matter, of death, no matter what the circumstance? To be "there" is for me such an incredible privilege.

◊

And so it is: Without seeking reward, we are rewarded. Without making personal blessing our focus, we find blessing in even the most painful encounters we experience.

Some who exercise their gift of compassion will find immediate rewards and instant gratification. Those rewards are the hugs, the verbal or physical pats on the back, or just words such as, "Thank you! Your presence helped so much."

For most of us, however, it is the long look back that allows us to see the full scope of blessing and reward. As the circumstances with which we find ourselves involved play out, we see how our being there and exercising compassion made a difference. Compassion shared solved a problem and created a long-term friendship. In its very expression, it affected spiritual change, and in that, people were helped and God was glorified.

For many of us, it may be that only eternity will tell, and only in eternity will we gain reward. While the earthly rewards may be more immediate and ego lifting, it is the eternal rewards that are "bankable" with God. The compassionate person may not see an immediate reward—or any earthly award at all—but in patience and in eternity the reward will come...*if* that is not our goal in expressing compassion.

The Reward of Acting on Behalf of God

The God of eternity has a mission on this earth and has called his followers to carry out that mission. He gifts and equips some with very public and noticeable abilities and some with ones that are quiet and barely noticeable. Whatever the gift, whatever the circumstance of its usage, all who exercise the gifts do so on behalf of God. To act on behalf of and in concert with the Creator, Sustainer, and Benefactor of all humanity— that is reward in itself.

In May 1985 I wrote

It is spelled P-R-O-V-I-D-E-N-T-I-A-L and it means, "Occurring as if by an act of God." It came boldly illustrated in my life this month in the form of a twenty-month-old little girl named Sarah.

A phone call took me to a street corner where I met Sarah and her daddy. Her hands and chubby little cheeks were red from the cold wind. Her big brown eyes, shy but imploring, stole my heart away and I said inside, "I must help!"

I heard a heartwrenching story of a mother who no longer wanted this little girl, a helpless father with no present means to support her, and I was on the phone looking for money for a bus ticket to Boston, where little Sarah's grandmother could help. Our emergency fund "provided" (sounds a little like providential) and I waved goodbye.

Now 7:30 a.m. is not a bad time in the morning...unless you are talking Boston time. That translates to 4:30 a.m. our time, and that's when my phone rang about ten days later. On the Acton, Massachusetts, end of the line was a hysterical, crying woman who turned out to be little Sarah's grandmother. Problems, and I'm 3,000 miles away. "There must be some resource for you there," was met by the plaintive cry, "But we don't have any police chaplains here!" A list of Acton pastors secured from the phone book would have to do.

The first phone call was answered by a janitor at the local brand X church. He would not give me the pastor's home phone number, sure that he would not want to be disturbed on Saturday. (I was just as sure that this pastor was not the resource I needed.) The next call was answered by an answering machine. "Oh, no!" I left a message and, feeling disheartened, gave up. Less than one hour later my phone rang from Acton again. It was the pastor with the answering machine! He listened intently to my request for assistance and said in a voice that sang in sweet melody over the phone, "Just last week I was named police chaplain for our city." PROVIDENTIAL! But the story does not end there.

I later learned that the chaplain had tried unsuccessfully to contact Sarah's daddy until he showed up at the police station a week later, desperate to talk with someone. "Do you have a police chaplain?" The pastor/chaplain called me from his office that day and "daddy" was there and they were getting it all worked out.

Providence (God) brings people together, and it is a thrill to see him at work. He works in both the life of the helper and that of the one who needs help.

❖

Providence has his providers. When he has a mission that requires compassion, he sends out compassionate missionaries. We, the missionaries, do not go alone. He goes with us. It is a mission on behalf of the King, and the King goes along. Not the king of England, not the king of Sweden, but the King of the whole of creation—of life itself.

To put on his badge and take on his identity is the reward. My good friend and fellow chaplain Art Sphar wrote it this way: "Where I go, Jesus goes. I'm just his chauffeur."

As Art and I talked about his role as one of our volunteers, he quickly began to recount a recent experience at the death of a three-month-old baby. Sudden Infant Death Syndrome (SIDS) was strongly suspected, and Art sought to comfort the very young mother who had just lost her baby. He described it as "the ultimate horror, every parent's worst nightmare." And indeed it is.

My question to Art was, "Why, Art? Why chaplaincy? Why you?" He dropped into a compassionate tone and told me, "I felt the grief and loss too. What can you do?" Then his words, "Where I go, Jesus goes."

This is Christianity at its best: "...Christ in you, the hope of glory" (Colossians 1:27). With that theology, it is "Where I go,

Jesus goes." In other words, he directs us and leads us and we follow, going in his name and with his presence. We are his ambassadors, those who act on his behalf being his hands, his feet, and his tongue, speaking his words of comfort and compassion.

It is reward in itself that with Jesus we live out his own words: "For I was hungry and you gave me something to eat, I was thirsty and you gave me something to drink, I was a stranger and you invited me in, I needed clothes and you clothed me, I was sick and you looked after me, I was in prison and you came to visit me" (Matthew 25:35-36).

In September 1990 I wrote

I have watched them descend into their private "hell" following the suicide death of their loved ones. The last two weekends have found me on the road to the southeast part of the county en route to gunshot suicides of young women. The first was thirty-five, the second only twenty-three.

I watched families slide off into that "hell" of the realization of what had happened and begin to question, "Why?" A part of the "hell" is to realize that suicide is truly a permanent solution to a temporary problem and to know that it can never be taken back. Their friend, daughter, wife, lover is forever and irreversibly gone from this earth, never to return.

To watch their turmoil, anguish, and pain is somehow obscene...as if you are a voyeur intruding upon people's most private moments. Yet you have to stand your ground watching the pain spread and incapacitate, waiting for the moment when they reach out to you, questioning pain in their eyes.

"The rich man also died and was buried. In hell, where he was in torment, he looked up and saw Abraham far away, with Lazarus by his side. So he called to him, 'Father Abraham, have pity on me and send Lazarus to dip the tip of his finger in water and cool my tongue, because I am in agony in this fire'" (Luke 16:22-24).

To those families in the torment of their "hell on earth," we can only come with the tip of our fingers dipped in cooling water. We as chaplains can provide some help for the moment until the "fire of grief" cools and finally dies. Because of the moments of help from the chaplain we hope and pray that, "Beauty will come from ashes" and they will find real relief in him.

❖

In acting on behalf of God, the compassionate One, we bring relief to the hopeless and the helpless. We become instrumental in delivering the food to the hungry, clothing to the naked, cold water to the thirsty—even if it's only dipping our finger in the water to cool the tongue of the tormented. And that is enough. It is reward in and of itself because we have acted on behalf of God.

The Reward of Sharing in His Sufferings

We rode out together on the shuttle to the San Antonio airport. She was dressed in casual slacks and blouse, and I would not have guessed she was a Catholic sister. I am of the generation that still expects every nun to be always dressed in a habit. I rarely have the opportunity to share with a person of such depth; it quickly became "brain-picking time." As I was already in the thinking mode of this chapter, my question to her was, "What do you get out of being a chaplain? What are the rewards?" Her answer should not have surprised me, but it did: "It is an opportunity to share in the sufferings of the Lord."

Sharing in a lot of things is very popular, but sharing in suffering is not. A part of the human condition is certainly good and pleasant. We see the healthy, the wealthy, the whole, and the happy. All of us want to share in that part. But most are not so willing to share in the other part: the ill, the poor, the broken, and the downcast. The popular conception of sharing in suffering is that it is generally left to those who spend their lives in khakis and pith helmets or flowing robes and Birkenstock sandals. For most of us, it's, "I will share your fortune, your good will, or your BMW, but I would rather leave the suffering to the Mother Teresa types."

In my area of ministry, it is the police officers and the firefighters who run *toward* suffering and danger while others run away. We pay them, as well as the doctors and nurses and homeless shelter workers, to take on the unpleasant, dirty, or dangerous tasks.

The rest of the world stays away—*gladly* stays away. But how many times do we read of the Lord moving toward the sick and the lame, the blind and the beggar? How many times have we read of him: "He was moved with compassion"? Over and over again, Jesus runs toward the needy. Today, he invites us to join him in this serving up of the other slice of life.

In our human minds, the suffering of Jesus is commonly assigned to the Cross, but it encompasses far more. It encompasses not just what he did *on* the Cross but *before* the Cross as well. Each time Scripture recounts, "He was moved with compassion," it is the suffering of the Cross. As he moves us to compassion, we get to experience and share the suffering he shared with the blind and broken, the hopeless and helpless. Each experience we share with him is *our* suffering of the Cross.

In the Mark 5 account, Jesus responds not to Jairus the ruler of the synagogue, but to "Daddy" Jairus, whose daughter has fallen ill and died. As Jesus and his disciples move toward Jairus's home on the mission of mercy, yet another one in need of compassion interrupts them. Jesus stops to help, and the woman is healed of her bleeding problem and blessed. And then Jesus, knowing that the little girl has died, moves on to-

ward the home where her father's family and friends are grieving, crying, and wailing over her loss. Who wants to be there
during a time of such agony and pain? Jesus does. He *chose* to
be a part of Jairus's suffering, and he bids us, invites us, and
urges us to do the same thing in our own circles today. When
we do, we are blessed to become a part of the suffering Jesus
takes on.

He invites us into the "fellowship of...his suffering"
(Philippians 3:10). While we cannot put suffering in a con-
tainer or by sharing it take a quarter or half of the weight of it
away, we *can* enter into deeper fellowship with Jesus and with
those who are suffering when we choose to share in it. While
one definition of "fellowship" might invite us to share Christ's
interest in those who suffer, the deeper, more meaningful,
more accurate definition would invite us into a *communion* of
suffering with him. It means to become one with him and to
actually partake in his suffering and the suffering of others. It
means to share the suffering as if it were our own, indeed to
make it our own. That communion is the true sharing of the
suffering.

In my role as a chaplain, I often tell those who are suffering, "I will be here with you. You will not have to do this
alone." This implication that I was willing to share the suffering—to mentally and spiritually take a part of it, to share the
tremendous load that has come down upon them—helped victims of crisis. In a very real sense, this created a bond because
we shared something: the uniqueness and the awfulness of the
experience.

The personal pain involved in sharing in this way is sometimes indescribable. But to enter into it on behalf of someone
else is another indescribable—an indescribable privilege.

On August 14, 1986, I wrote

My special day dawned bright with an easy sort of day in the works...friends over for dinner, happy birthday sung, some gifts (I hoped), and the usual birthday cake.

But Oh God, why? He was so little!

Only a few moments of carelessness on the part of the babysitter and the baby was dead...suffocated by the pillows of the couch, pressed tight by the sleeping babysitter's body.

The word came just as I left to get started toward home: "They are asking for a chaplain. Are you available?" "Try the district chaplain," I answered. "If he isn't I will respond." He wasn't and I did.

We waited for the mother to arrive. One of our deputies had met her going ninety miles per hour on the freeway and he had brought her to the scene. We caught her as she slipped to the pavement in shock as I told her—oh, how I hate that part. We somehow got through it and reinforcements began to arrive.

It wasn't until I started home, hurrying not to miss my birthday dinner, that I remembered her words: "I had just taken him to the doctor this morning for his one-year checkup."

Oh God, could it have been this little guy's birthday too? "Why me, Lord? Why do I get forty-seven years? Let me go home grateful for all you have given me of life and health and peace."

❖

As we go to the place of the suffering person, whether it is physical or emotional pain, we go with Christ and together we share the suffering.

At the end of my chaplaincy career I wrote: "What wonderful privileges I have had in life because of being a chaplain. How much poorer my life would have been without these privileges...some of them very painful privileges." As it is a privilege to go with him to the place of suffering, so is it a privilege to share the suffering.

The Reward of Seeing Beauty Rise from Ashes

Whether you prefer the simple but poetic words of the King James Version or the more explanatory words of the New International Version, you can find this hope-filled message in the Old Testament book of Isaiah: "...to comfort all who mourn, and to provide for those who grieve in Zion—to bestow on them a crown of beauty instead of ashes, the oil of gladness instead of mourning..." (Isaiah 61:2-3).

In ancient Jewish culture, those who mourned often poured ashes upon their heads as a symbol to all that tragedy had befallen them. The promise from Isaiah's book is that in mourning God will provide a crown of beauty—perhaps of jewels or gold—or even a headdress of fragrant blossoms to replace the ashes.

We often wonder about the meaning of this promise, but since I first read it, and then began to live it, it has produced a day-to-day hope that finds its echo in Romans 8:28: "And we know that in all things God works for the good of those who love him, who have been called according to his purpose."

The explosion of Mount Saint Helens in 1980 provides a graphic illustration of beauty from ashes and good coming out of bad. This disaster ripped down trees, incinerated people and countless animals, and spread smothering ash across hundreds, if not thousands, of square miles. From the terrible devastation wrought by the eruption of this volcano that graced the skyline of the Pacific Northwest came something beautiful. Glass artisans took the volcanic ash and from it made beautiful glass objects. This glass has an especially beautiful and distinct hue; it was used to make art for many to preserve and treasure.

How like the promise of God, "beauty instead of ashes!" It is as if the Father says, "I can take the worst thing that could ever happen and bring from it something so surprising and so beautiful that you will be stunned into submission to me."

Virtually every day of my ministry, as I was confronted by grief and tragedy, I clung desperately to these promises: "Beauty for ashes...oil of joy for mourning...in all things God works for the good of those who love him." They were my mantra, my life-savers, my link to the Father during the darkest hours. They fueled the engine of compassion within me and gave me courage to face yet another dark moment with yet another victim.

These promises answered for me this question from the man whose eighteen-month-old son lay dead in his filthy bed: "Do you believe in a God who would let a little boy like that die?" They were the answer to the woman whose husband was a homicide victim. In the midst of crisis, they were a private answer for me alone. It was yet too early to speak such words to victim families, but I could drive away each time, consoled within myself and willing to wait until God made plain for all to see that good could come from every bad situation.

The good did not make it OK that the bad had happened. The good did not suddenly transform evil to good or wrong to right. It did not lessen the loss of a child or make a suicide the solution to the problem. But these promises helped make sense out of tragedy and bring about something that never would have happened if the tragedy had not struck.

These promises often motivated me to keep going day after day, and even rejoice, after tragedy struck, knowing that God had a special responsibility for me and others who responded.

We would be the instruments through which the beauty would come about, ambassadors of the Lord to assist in the creation of beauty.

The Reward of an Opened and Meaningful Life

Down through the generations, the lessons of life have been written in the valleys. Human nature seems to be well fitted with this life principle: the deeper the valley the more valuable the lesson. When we learn our lessons in those valleys, we curse ourselves for not being willing to learn the lesson from the mountaintop, realizing only then how much easier it would have been.

Jesus' encounter with the so-called "rich young ruler," juxtaposed with his encounter with the blind beggar who would not stop shouting and begging for mercy, provides a worthy example. The one who "had it all" was not happy, and the one who was blind and dependent upon alms for his daily bread would not stop shouting out his need and voicing his helplessness. The one went away sorrowful, and the other left the scene shouting for joy.

Likewise, in the moment of poverty and loneliness one we have come to call the Prodigal Son learned a valuable lesson—learned what life was really all about. After he learned the lesson the hard way, he returned home to his father, the man who just months before seemed like such an old "stick in the mud."

So it is with us. Compassionate ones find themselves deliberately choosing to enter the crucible and be "ground up." In that grinding and pounding we learn life's most valuable lessons and we discover the true meaning of life.

I am in Estonia as I write this section of the book. It is a beautiful country that knows well the meaning of freedom, not because it has been free for many years but because it has not.

The true meaning of freedom is so deeply imbedded in the Estonian people's heads and hearts only because they learned it through the contrast of decades spent under the heavy and brutal hand of Communism.

Likewise, the meaning of life comes to us as we look death squarely in the face. The meaning of joy comes when we have endured the depths of sorrow and grief. These kinds of contrasts sharpen our focus, allowing us to clearly see the value of the hard things that have been a part of our lives.

It is in that realization that we can praise God in all things. In that realization I look back on my own life and find my early childhood to have been an asset to my adult life. In that realization I can cast away all thoughts of anger or bitterness, which may well be the natural consequence of such a childhood. I can know that God has used each part of my life's experience, not only to make me who I am but to glorify himself in my life.

For some reason it took me fifty years to figure it out. It is not the quantity of life that gives it meaning, it is quality. Real meaning is accomplished in a short time if one lives compassionately, sensitively, and with caring and concern.

The compassionate life is lived in shoulder-rubbing closeness to those who are experiencing the contrasts of joy and sorrow, pain and pleasure, and even life and death. We learn what it means to be in fellowship with another human being. The fellowship, the bonding, and the closeness come when we truly share experiences.

The compassionate one—the one who is drawn to those who suffer—indeed walks with God where God walks, shares the pain of the Cross, and through it all, discovers himself or herself and the true meaning of life. That is joy unspeakable. That is the reward of compassion.

Bibliography

Jones, E. Stanley. *The Christ of the Mount*. Nashville: Abingdon Press, 1931.

Nouwen, Henri. *Compassion: A Reflection on the Christian Life*. New York: Image Books/Doubleday, 1983.

Nouwen, Henri. *The Wounded Healer*. New York: Doubleday, 1972.

Dan Nolta

Dan has been an emergency services chaplain since 1971. He began this ministry by volunteering with the Tacoma (Washington) Police Department, where he served until 1977. He also ministered four years as a volunteer chaplain with the Tacoma Fire Department before he started his full-time service with the Pierce County Sheriff's Department (PCSD) in 1984.

Besides coordinating the PCSD chaplaincy program, Dan has been president and now serves as international liaison for the International Conference of Police Chaplains (ICPC). This assignment was given him after he traveled extensively to other countries to review police agencies and chaplaincy programs.

In his nearly 20 years with Tacoma-Pierce County Chaplaincy and in his assignment as chaplain coordinator for the Pierce County Sheriff's Department, he has twice been called upon to serve as interim executive director. During his years with Tacoma-Pierce County Chaplaincy, the organization has expanded to the point that it now provides chaplaincy services for some 30 emergency services agencies in Pierce County.

Dan, who attained a Master level of training with the ICPC, greatly values the training he has received, and educating other chaplains has long been one of his passions. Under the sponsorship of Tacoma-Pierce County Chaplaincy, Dan founded the

Police and Fire Chaplain's Training Academy in partnership with the Washington State Criminal Justice Training Commission. The academy is designed to give emergency services chaplains basic knowledge to be equipped to serve effectively. In addition to local training experiences, Dan was privileged to conduct the first ICPC-sponsored training outside North America when he assisted in educating African police chaplains in Kenya in 2004.

Retired from active chaplaincy in December 2004, Dan continues to serve as ICPC international liaison. He also spends time consulting and writing grants for Tacoma-Pierce County Chaplaincy, fishing, and enjoying his family.

CPSIA information can be obtained at www.ICGtesting.com
Printed in the USA
BVOW05s0320210814

362992BV00016B/16/A